FAITHFUL
LARGE PRINT EDITION

Faithful:
Christmas Through the Eyes of Joseph

Faithful

978-1-5018-1408-2 *Hardcover with jacket*

978-1-5018-1409-9 *eBook*

978-1-5018-1410-5 *Large Print*

Faithful: DVD

978-1-5018-1402-0

Faithful: Leader Guide

978-1-5018-1411-2

978-1-5018-1412-9 *eBook*

Faithful: Youth Study Book

978-1-5018-1413-6

978-1-5018-1414-3 *eBook*

Faithful: Children's Leader Guide

978-1-5018-1415-0

Also from Adam Hamilton

24 Hours That Changed the World

Christianity and World Religions

Christianity's Family Tree

Confronting the Controversies

Creed

Enough

Final Words from the Cross

Forgiveness

Half Truths

John

Leading Beyond the Walls

Love to Stay

Making Sense of the Bible

Moses

Not a Silent Night

Revival

Seeing Gray in a World of Black and White

Selling Swimsuits in the Arctic

Speaking Well

The Call

The Journey

The Way

Unafraid

Unleashing the Word

When Christians Get It Wrong

Why?

For more information, visit www.AdamHamilton.org.

ADAM HAMILTON

FAITHFUL

CHRISTMAS THROUGH THE EYES OF
JOSEPH

LARGE PRINT EDITION

Abingdon Press / Nashville

FAITHFUL:
CHRISTMAS THROUGH THE EYES OF JOSEPH
LARGE PRINT EDITION

This book is printed on elemental chlorine-free paper.
978-1-5018-1410-5

17 18 19 20 21 22 23 24 25 26—10 9 8 7 6 5 4 3 2 1
MANUFACTURED IN THE UNITED STATES OF AMERICA

Dedicated to all of the children
who are refugees and orphans in our world today.
100 percent of the royalties from this book
will go to projects benefiting these children.

CONTENTS

1

A CARPENTER
NAMED JOSEPH

When he came to his hometown, he taught the people in their synagogue. They were surprised and said, "Where did he get this wisdom? Where did he get the power to work miracles? Isn't he the carpenter's son? Isn't his mother named Mary? Aren't James, Joseph, Simon, and Judas his brothers? And his sisters, aren't they here with us? Where did this man get all this?"

(Matthew 13:54-56)

1

A CARPENTER
NAMED JOSEPH

Typically when Christians explore the stories surrounding the birth of Jesus—often during the Advent season—they focus on Mary, the mother of Jesus, and on Luke's account of the Christmas story, which is told from her vantage point. But in this little book our focus will be on Joseph, his life, and his role in the birth and life of Jesus. And that means our biblical focus will be on Matthew's account of Christmas, which is told from Joseph's vantage point.

No man played a more important role in Jesus' life than Joseph. Though not Jesus' biological father, Joseph adopted Jesus as his son. Joseph protected him, provided for him, taught and mentored him.

We don't often hear about Joseph because there is rel-atively little in the Gospels about him. They contain only a handful of stories about him around the time of Jesus' birth, and a couple of references to Jesus as "Joseph's son" later in the Gospels (the Gospel of Mark doesn't mention him at all). Nor will you find anything about him in the Acts of the Apostles or any of the Epistles.

So we have to read between the lines to fill in the picture of Joseph's life, and to some extent we must use our imagination to connect the bits of information we do find in the Gospels. As we do this, we will find that there's more than meets the eye in the New Testament accounts of Joseph's life.

Though the story of Joseph speaks to everyone, I believe it may speak in particularly important ways to fathers, husbands, stepfathers, grandfathers, and men who have the opportunity to mentor others.

As I've been writing this book, I've been asking some basic questions:

- What can we learn about God from Joseph's story?
- What can we learn about ourselves from Joseph's story?
- How does Joseph shed light on the meaning of the Christmas story?

Joseph in the Early Church

Beginning in the second century, Christians found themselves longing for more information than we find in the Gospels about Jesus' childhood and parents. Some Christians sought to fill in the gaps by writing what scholars call the apocryphal gospels. *Apocrypha* is a Greek word that means obscure or hidden. When we describe a story today as apocryphal, we mean that we don't really know whether it is true.

While Matthew, Mark, Luke, and John were written in the second half of the first century—between AD 65 and 90—the apocryphal gospels came much later; the earliest seem to have been written around AD 150, and some of them date as late as the fifth century. In other words, the earliest of these books were written approximately 150 years after Jesus was born. Authorship of these "hidden gospels" is usually attributed to a New Testament figure, James or Mary or Peter or Thomas, though the books were written long after these people had died.

Many stories in the apocryphal gospels are fanciful and completely out of character with the Jesus we meet in Matthew, Mark, Luke, and John. Still, it is possible that occasionally some of the apocryphal gospels preserved traditions that were historical, stories that had been passed down by the church but not included in the canonical gospels.

For example, the Infancy Gospel of Thomas (not to be confused with the Gospel of Thomas) is thought to have been written around AD 150. It is a collection of short stories purporting to be about Jesus' life from age five to age twelve, including the story also told in Luke about Jesus being accidentally left by his parents in Jerusalem. The Infancy Gospel of Thomas contains a much larger role for Joseph than we find in the New Testament Gospels. In it, we find Joseph sending Jesus to school to be educated, not common among the children of first-century woodworkers. Joseph attempts to discipline Jesus (grabbing him by the ear at one point!) and often attempts to help Jesus use his powers wisely.

The Infancy Gospel of James (sometimes known as the Protoevangelium of James or simply the Gospel of James) is also thought to have been written around AD 150. It claims to have been written by James, whom the Gospels refer to as one of the brothers of Christ. The book gives us the earliest account of Mary's birth, her childhood, and a particular account of Joseph's age when he married Mary. It suggests that Mary was raised by the priests in the temple courts from the age of three until she was twelve. According to this apocryphal gospel, the priests sought a husband for Mary among the older widowers from the House of David, with the intention that she be cared for by her husband as a father might care for his daughter or a grandfather for his granddaughter.

As the widowers gathered, each was given a rod or stick. Joseph, himself an elderly widower, took one of these rods, and from it a dove sprang forth and landed on Joseph's head. (Other versions have flowers bloom from the rod.) Hence the priests knew that Joseph was chosen by God to be Mary's husband. The account is legendary, as are many of the stories found in the apocryphal gospels. It is the earliest depiction of Joseph as an elderly widower when he became engaged to Mary. This depiction allowed Christians to read about Jesus' brothers and sisters in the New Testament Gospels as if they were Joseph's children by a previous wife, and hence Jesus' half-siblings.

If we had only the New Testament Gospels of Matthew and Luke to go by, we would not necessarily think of Joseph as an elderly widower. The accounts don't preclude this, but they don't suggest it either. Instead, if this engagement were a typical engagement we would imagine that Mary was thirteen or fourteen when she got married (remember, in ancient Israel a girl became a woman with her first menstrual cycle and was married shortly after that) and that Joseph was only a little older. Boys were required to have apprenticed under their fathers and be able to support themselves and a family before they married. So, if Joseph were not an elderly widower, we would suppose he may have been fourteen, fifteen, or perhaps sixteen when he "took Mary as his wife" (Matthew 1:24).

Yet the story of Joseph as an elderly widower took hold in the church. Sometime around the sixth century, a document called *The History of Joseph the Carpenter* was compiled, consisting of traditions concerning the Holy Family.* In the document, Joseph was said to be ninety years old when his first wife died, leaving him with six children to raise. Not only was Joseph described as a carpenter, but, because of his piety and wisdom, the legend had developed that he'd also been a priest. This apocryphal account said that a year after his first wife's death, Joseph was chosen to become the husband of Mary. Two years later, during a betrothal period when a couple was regarded as married but could not yet consummate their relationship (you'll learn more about that in chapter 2), Mary became pregnant. It was then that Joseph formally married her, which would have

---

* We're not sure when this work was written. Some suggest as early as the fifth century, others as late as the seventh century.

made him ninety-three when Jesus was born. According to this story, Joseph died at the age of one hundred eleven, when Jesus was eighteen.

Legends such as this built upon one another and shaped the view that many in the church had of Joseph. Whether this story is true or not, it supported an idea that began emerging with the church's deepening devotion to Mary—namely, that she was perpetually a virgin and never consummated her marriage to Joseph. By the fourth century this view was commonly held, and even today it is an official doctrine of the Catholic Church. But Catholics were far from the only Christians who believed it; Eastern Orthodox churches subscribed to it, as did Martin Luther and most of the Protestant Reformers. To my surprise, I discovered that even John Wesley, the eighteenth-century founder of Methodism, held this view.[1]

Today, many Protestants reject the idea that Mary remained a virgin for life, or that Joseph was an elderly widower. They view Joseph as a young man when he married Mary and believe that the brothers and sisters of Jesus mentioned in the Gospels (see Matthew 12:47; 13:55-56; Mark 6:3; and others) were the biological children of Mary and Joseph, Jesus' younger siblings. If we discount the early church traditions about Joseph's age and the need to insist that Mary was perpetually a virgin, a younger Joseph seems to make the most sense to me. As I pointed out, the Gospels can be read to support either of these views.

Joseph in Classical Art

We can see these two different views by looking at classical images of Joseph, particularly in Renaissance and later art. In the early 1600s, Italian artist Guido Reni painted several famous images of "St. Joseph and the Christ Child" that portrayed Joseph as an elderly man holding the infant Jesus in a loving embrace. The contrast in age can be seen clearly in two images from the Baroque era that are shown on the next page. In "The Holy Family with Dog," Spanish painter Bartolomé Esteban Murillo showed Joseph as a young, vigorous father; whereas in "St. Joseph with the Infant Jesus," Italian painter and printmaker Elisabetta Sirani portrayed Joseph as an older man.

I've encouraged my congregation to look at their Nativity sets at home to see how Joseph is portrayed. Many portray Joseph as an elderly man, though some, particularly those created by Protestant artists, show him to be quite young.

"The Holy Family with Dog"
by Bartolomé Esteban Murillo

"St. Joseph with the Infant
Jesus" by Elisabetta Sirani

So, Joseph was either an aged widower who had children by a previous wife, or he was a fourteen-to-eighteen-year-old youth who had other children with Mary after the birth of Jesus. If all we had were the New Testament Gospel accounts—absent the early church's conviction that Mary must have remained perpetually a virgin (built upon the idea, it seems, that sexual intimacy with Joseph in the years after Jesus' birth would have diminished her in some way)—I believe most would conclude that Joseph was a young man when Jesus was born. But again, the Gospel accounts of Joseph and

Mary are not incompatible with the view that Joseph was an elderly widower. I leave it to the reader to decide.

Joseph the Carpenter

In Matthew 13:54-56, Jesus returned to his hometown of Nazareth, and some were offended by his teaching. They asked, "Isn't he the carpenter's son? Isn't his mother named Mary? Aren't James, Joseph, Simon, and Judas his brothers? And his sisters, aren't they here with us? Where did this man get all this?"

Mary is named in this passage, as are the brothers. The sisters are not named, but it is mentioned that they were living in Nazareth. Joseph, the earthly father of Jesus, is not named, likely indicating that by the time Jesus was pursuing his ministry, Joseph had died. Nevertheless, Joseph's occupation was remembered and mentioned: he was the carpenter.

The people expressed surprise at Jesus, and not in a good way. You can almost hear the snide tone when they asked: "Where did he get this wisdom? Where did he get the power to work miracles? Isn't he the carpenter's son?" (vv. 54-55). The mention of his father's profession seems clearly aimed at discrediting Jesus, saying in effect, "How can a lowly carpenter's son have such wisdom and power?"

In Mark's Gospel, by the way, the people described Jesus not as a carpenter's son but as a carpenter himself. That tells us that Jesus was trained by Joseph to follow in his trade. It seems likely that Jesus worked as a carpenter, first in his father's shop and then on his own, from the time he was a small boy until his baptism at age thirty.

If Joseph was a carpenter (and in turn Jesus as well), let's consider what that tells us about him. The Greek word translated as carpenter is *tekton*. The word can mean a variety of things, but it seems most often to have meant someone who worked with wood. Because wood was in short supply in Galilee, the area where Jesus grew up and conducted most of his ministry, most houses there were built of stone or mud brick. Though a *tekton* could be a house builder, there was a different word in Greek specifically for stonemasons. Someone who worked with wood would have made the doors and shutters for a house. But it is likely that much of the work of a *tekton* involved building furniture, chests, and tables along with farm implements, tools, and yokes for oxen.

Greek also had a word for master builders—*architekton*—from which we get the word architect. An *architekton* was a master craftsman and usually had others working for him. But Joseph was described in

Matthew not as an *architekton*, a master builder, merely as a *tekton*.

At home I have an old toolbox filled with tools that belonged to my great-grandfather. He was named Joseph, after Joseph the earthly father of Jesus, and he was also a carpenter. I love these old woodworking tools. Some of them, like his plane and chisel, are not very different from the tools used in the time of Jesus. Every once in a while, I take one of those old tools out of that toolbox and use it, just to feel connected with my great-grandfather. He was a giant of a man. Though I was a boy when he died, I can picture his huge hands and white hair, and I can still see him sitting in a rocking chair at my grandmother's house. When I picture him in my mind, I can also picture Joseph.

Not long ago, I went to Unruh Furniture in Kansas City, where about twenty men and women, most in their twenties and thirties, build beautiful handcrafted furniture. They are modern-day *tektons*. I sat down and talked with a couple of them, wondering what insight they might have about Joseph, given that Joseph, like them, had built furniture and other things.

One told me, "I would say Joseph was a man's man. He was probably way tougher than anyone that works here. I don't think he would have taken any shortcuts. I think he would have been patient. I think he would have been kind." Another noted, "He was likely smart, diligent, a good teacher, just striving to do something well....All of those things that he needed in order to be a carpenter, you know, translate well into actually being a father."

A document written about AD 150 by an early church leader we know as Justin Martyr says that Jesus "was in the habit of working as a carpenter when among men, making ploughs and yokes."[2] Unlike the writers of the apocryphal gospels, Justin Martyr is a very trustworthy source. Martyr's description of Jesus, pointing also to Joseph's work, gives added meaning to Jesus' words in Matthew 11:28-30 (NRSV):

> *"Come to me, all you that are weary and are carrying heavy burdens, and I will give you rest. Take my yoke upon you, and learn from me; for I am gentle and humble in heart, and you will find rest for your souls. For my yoke is easy, and my burden is light."*

Joseph, Jesus, and You

What does it tell us about God that he chose Joseph to serve as Jesus' earthly father and raise Jesus as his own son? Why didn't God choose a priest, an educated scribe or lawyer, a physician or successful businessman, or even an *architekton*? Why did he entrust the job to a humble carpenter?

You may remember the wonderful story (1 Samuel 16:1-13) in which, a thousand years before the birth of Jesus, God sent Samuel to Bethlehem to anoint one of Jesse's sons to be Israel's next king. Jesse brought out the oldest, tallest, strongest, and most handsome of his sons and Samuel thought, He must be the one! Yet God said, "Not that one." Jesse brought forth his second-oldest son, and once more God said, "Not that one." Jesse did this with all but one of his sons. Finally, when God had rejected all the other sons, Samuel asked, "Do you have any more sons?" Jesse said there was one more, his youngest son, David, who was out tending the sheep.

Samuel demanded to see David, and when David was brought in, God said to Samuel, "He's the one!" God said to Samuel, "The LORD does not see as mortals see; they look on the outward appearance, but the LORD looks on the heart" (v. 7 NRSV). In the end, the one chosen was, by outward appearances, the least impressive of Jesse's sons—the youngest and scrawniest. With Joseph, God continued that pattern, looking at the heart and choosing an unlikely hero for the important mission of raising the Messiah.

How Have Your Father, Stepfather, or Other Men in Your Life Shaped You?

Only sixteen verses in the Bible (NRSV) mention Joseph by name, but I believe his influence was much stronger and wider than you might guess from those few passages. I would argue that almost everything you read in the Gospels about what Jesus said and did was shaped at least in part by Joseph.

Fathers play an enormous role in shaping our lives. For some of us, that role is powerful, positive, and beautiful; for others, it may have been difficult and painful. However our fathers shaped us, we are their children in ways we may not fully realize.

I asked my friends on Facebook how they had been shaped by their fathers, and I received a wonderful array of answers. A handful of those who responded noted that their fathers were absent from their lives or were abusive or otherwise missed the mark as dads. Of course, even these experiences, placed in God's hands, can be redeemed. Some of the most compassionate and amazing dads I know had fathers who were absent from their lives, which led them to a dogged determination to be available and present in their children's lives.

But though some had fathers who missed the mark, I heard from many others who described remarkable dads. Here are just a few of the comments about dads, and lessons learned from them, that touched me.

> My dad taught me by word and example to never stop learning and always be there for your child. He passed away eleven years ago. Not a day goes by that I don't think of him.

> My dad taught me that a smart man will always admit when he is wrong.

> My dad embodied compassion. He taught me and modeled for me what it means to truly care for and love others.

> My dad taught me honesty and integrity—he did it by example. You could take his word to the bank.

> My dad was the model of courage as he lived with the effects of polio he contracted when he was three.

> My dad was a former boxer and he taught me, "You gotta roll with the punches" and "You gotta bob and weave," which is what I've done throughout my life.

> My father believed our place on earth was to help others and to take care of those who are weak or too small to defend themselves....I have never questioned how I became a social worker, having been my father's daughter.

Many noted how their fathers profoundly shaped their own faith. One seventy-eight-year-old member of our congregation told me, "I'm in church today because my dad insisted on taking me to Sunday school and worship every Sunday as I was growing up, and somehow it stuck."

My dad reads my Facebook page, just as many parents read their children's pages. Seeing that I had asked people about their fathers, he asked, How had he, as my father, shaped my life?

My answer: Dad, you were driven when I was growing up. You worked harder than anyone I know in order to succeed and get ahead, and you accomplished a lot. You are a pretty amazing guy, and from you I gained the drive to succeed. I gained a desire to give everything to whatever I am doing, and I learned about leadership from you.

As I was growing up, my dad spent a lot of time at work—he was a workaholic, putting in sixty to seventy hours a week. I remember thinking, as a kid, "When I have children of my own, I'll try not to work quite so many hours, so I can spend more time with them." But as my children were growing up, I found myself wrestling with the same tendency. It seemed that I had become my dad.

My father's question also made me think of my stepfather. My parents divorced when I was a boy, and my mother remarried. So I learned from my stepdad, too. Like Joseph, he was a carpenter. He was a giant of a man—six feet five inches tall and 250 pounds and strong as an ox. Once he accidentally shot himself in the leg with a nail gun. He grabbed a pair of pliers, pulled the sixteen-penny nail out of his leg, and kept working the rest of the day.

Another time, when I was fourteen, my younger sister Dena did something to irritate me, as younger siblings often do. I responded that I was going to "get" her. My stepdad heard this. He lifted me up over his head— at the time I was almost six feet tall and weighed about 165 pounds—and said, "You don't ever threaten a woman." It scared the daylights out of me, and I never forgot it. Yet sometimes, when he was drinking, he forgot it. Part of what I learned from being his stepson was that you never hurt a woman, but I also learned that I don't ever want to be an alcoholic.

We learn from observing our dads. As I look back, a lot of the good things that happened in my life are because of my dad or my stepdad. But I also learned from them some things about what I didn't want to be or do. I suspect it's the same with most of us.

In a blog post, Lee Strobel, author of the book *The Case for Grace*, cited New York University psychologist Paul Vitz's work. Vitz wrote, "That a child's psychological representation of his father is intimately connected to his understanding of God was assumed by Freud and has been rather well developed by a number of psychologists, especially psychoanalysts."[3]

This makes sense, as I think most of us can recognize. Our relationship with our dad has something to do with how we picture God. If we have a healthy, loving relationship with our earthly father, then it's easier to have a good relationship with God. And if we have a relationship with our dad that is dysfunctional, then it can be harder to trust that God is a good and loving father.

Paul Vitz listed many noted atheists who had difficult relationships with their fathers, writing, "Disappointment in and resentment of his own father unconsciously justifies his rejection of God."[4] He wasn't suggesting that this was true in every case. Some atheists had great dads and great relationships with them.

Still, after reading what Vitz had written, Lee Strobel couldn't help wondering about the implications for our society. We live in a time when 26 percent of millennials say they have poor or below-average relationships with their fathers.[5] Is there a connection between this statistic and the number of millennials, particularly young men, who are struggling with the idea of faith in God?

The question takes me back to Joseph and Jesus. Jesus clearly had a great relationship with his heavenly father, and perhaps that points toward the kind of relationship he had with his earthly father, Joseph. When Jesus told his followers to address God as *Abba*, a word that meant something like "Dad," I wonder if he was also telling us that he saw in Joseph the heart and character of God.

Seeing Joseph in Jesus

Though the Gospels provide very little direct information about Joseph, I believe we can learn a lot about him by looking at his son. As I read the stories of Jesus, it appears to me that Joseph was intentional about teaching and modeling for Jesus who God is and what God's will was for his life.

When Jesus told the parable of the prodigal son—likening God to the patient and merciful father who took back his son even after the boy had demanded his inheritance in advance and then squandered everything on wild living—had Jesus seen this kind of love and forgiveness by Joseph in response to one or more of his brothers?

When Jesus spoke about the importance of telling the truth, might he have been describing what he had learned by watching Joseph?

When Jesus taught his disciples that true greatness is found in humble service, might he have been describing what he had seen in his carpenter father every single day?

When Jesus said we're not to look at a woman with lust in our hearts, was he repeating what he had learned from Joseph as a teen? Doesn't that sound like something a dad might tell his son when the son is thirteen or fourteen?

When Jesus said we should do to others what we want them to do to us, is it possible he had grown up seeing this value embodied by his earthly dad, both in Joseph's business and in his personal life?

Jesus undoubtedly learned many things from his mother, but I have to believe that much of what we see in Jesus reflected the life and witness of Joseph.

When I think about Joseph's story, what strikes me is that the person whose birth we celebrate at Christmas was in large part shaped by his human father (or stepfather, or adoptive father, or foster father—each of these terms might fit). It seems likely to me that Joseph intentionally taught and modeled love, faith, and fatherhood, and that what Jesus learned from him shaped his life and ministry.

How Do Others See Jesus (and Joseph) in You?

How are you shaping the children entrusted to your care? These might be your own children or grandchildren. If you don't have children these might be nieces or nephews, young people in the workplace, children in Sunday school or youth group. It's an important question for us all, but I think it is particularly important for men. What are you teaching about life to the children who look up to you? What image of God are you painting for them? When you die, what will your children and grandchildren, or other children, say they learned from you? What lessons will they continue to carry with them?

None of us has been asked to do what Joseph did in raising the Messiah. But every mother, father, step-mother, stepfather, grandma and grandpa, aunt and uncle has been asked to raise children of God, to show them a picture of God's love and mercy, and to teach them intentionally what it means to be God's children.

When we do that, we follow the example of a righteous man, Joseph of Nazareth.

God, how grateful we are to you for Joseph. Thank you for the model he presents to us, a model of how we're meant to pass on our faith to our children. Help us to be models of your love. Amen.

2

WHOSE CHILD IS THIS?

This is how the birth of Jesus Christ took place. When Mary his mother was engaged to Joseph, before they were married, she became pregnant by the Holy Spirit. Joseph her husband was a righteous man. Because he didn't want to humiliate her, he decided to call off their engagement quietly.

(Matthew 1:18-19)

2

WHOSE CHILD IS THIS?

Matthew's account of Joseph's story, and through it Jesus' story, begins with a scandal. With brevity and directness Matthew tells the reader that, while Joseph and Mary were engaged, Mary became pregnant and Joseph was not the father. Matthew leaves to the reader to ponder just how upsetting Mary's pregnancy must have been to Joseph. We don't learn the implications or legal consequences of what appeared to Joseph to be an act of infidelity, but we do get a hint of Joseph's character when we read his response to this news.

We as Christians know that Mary was not unfaithful, but Joseph did not know that. In this chapter we'll consider his thoughts, feelings, and actions in the hours before a messenger of the Lord appeared to him in a dream to confirm that the child in Mary's womb was from the Holy Spirit.

First, though, let's consider the part of Matthew's Gospel that precedes this story, a part that is often overlooked. Let's consider the genealogy of Jesus.

The Genealogy of Jesus

The first sixteen verses of Matthew's Gospel give us Jesus' family tree. We typically skip over these because their importance is not immediately apparent. Somebody begat somebody, who begat somebody. Some years ago *Reader's Digest*, famous for creating condensed versions of books, published *The Reader's Digest Bible*. In their abridged edition, the Old Testament was 55 percent shorter than the Bible we use, and the New Testament was 20 percent shorter. One part of the New Testament story that was left out entirely was the genealogy of Jesus as traced through Joseph.

Yet Matthew begins with Jesus' genealogy for a reason. For Matthew, recounting Jesus' lineage—his ancestors—tells us something about how God works and foreshadows Jesus' life and ministry. One reason his ancestry is included is to establish that Jesus was in fact a descendant of David and hence eligible to be the

Messiah. In 2 Samuel 7:16 God had sworn to David, "Your dynasty and your kingdom will be secured forever before me. Your throne will be established forever." Jews understood this to mean that when God sent the Messiah, the king God would raise up to liberate the Jewish people and to rule over them, this messianic king would be a descendant of David.

Yet Matthew begins his genealogy of Jesus not with David but with Abraham. (Luke begins his genealogy all the way back with Adam and Eve!) Why does Matthew begin with Abraham? In part it's because the Jewish people all considered themselves descendants of Abraham. But I wonder if it might also have been because of God's promise to Abraham in Genesis 12:3:

I will bless those who bless you,
those who curse you I will curse;
all the families of the earth
will be blessed because of you.

For Matthew, Jesus is the fulfillment of that promise. We see this blessing of all the nations in Jesus' final words in Matthew 28:19-20: "Go and make disciples of all nations, baptizing them in the name of the Father and of the Son and of the Holy Spirit, teaching them to obey everything that I've commanded you." Through

Jesus and his great commission—and through those who follow Jesus today—God's promise to Abraham is fulfilled.

One interesting thing about Matthew's tracing of Jesus' genealogy is that Matthew himself is giving us a condensed, "Reader's Digest" version. He leaves out multiple generations. How do we know? Because we can find passages with genealogies of these ancestors of Jesus in the Old Testament. For some reason, Matthew doesn't include all the generations.

However, Matthew makes a point of adding four names to the family tree of Joseph and Jesus that might easily have been left out of the genealogy. All these additions, significantly, were women. In those days, it was not customary (though not unheard of) to include women in a Jewish genealogy. Here, too, Matthew is not acting at random. He wants to make an important point about how God has worked in the past, and how that foreshadows how God will work in the life of Jesus.

Matthew could have included women whose names were familiar because they were wives and mothers of the patriarchs of Israel. But he didn't list Sarah (the wife of Abraham) or Rebecca (the wife of Isaac) or Rachel and Leah (the sisters who were wives of Jacob). Instead, Matthew lists Tamar, Rahab, Ruth, and Bathsheba (whom Matthew does not name but describes as "the wife of Uriah"). What makes the inclusion of these four women especially noteworthy is their unusual stories.

Tamar, whose story we find in Genesis, was forced to play the part of a prostitute in order to have children after her husband died. Rahab was a prostitute in Jericho who helped the Israelites as they were beginning to take the Promised Land. Ruth was a Moabite woman, a foreigner who lost her husband but ultimately won the heart of Boaz, an older man who was willing to accept this widowed foreigner as his wife. (Actually, all four of these women probably were foreigners.) And Bathsheba was the wife of Uriah the Hittite, one of King David's most loyal officers. While her husband, Uriah, was away at war fighting on the king's behalf, David summoned Bathsheba to the palace, where he initiated what at best was an adulterous relationship with her and at worst may have been rape. David then proceeded to have Bathsheba's husband killed.

I recently read Ron Chernow's bestselling book *Alexander Hamilton*, the basis of the hit Broadway musical *Hamilton*. Chernow begins by describing Alexander Hamilton's lineage, noting how Hamilton was said by his detractors to be an illegitimate son of an immoral mother. Chernow notes that Hamilton "never outgrew the stigma of his illegitimacy."[1] The story of Jesus' birth, like the stories of these four women in his lineage, would be considered by many to have been marks of illegitimacy.

Each of these four women knew pain, brokenness, and hardship. In one way or another, each had been scorned as unclean or as a sinner and shamed by people in their communities. But ultimately God used them, blessed them, and blessed their offspring, and they became a part of God's redemptive work in the world.

Perhaps this genealogy was intended to prepare us, the readers of Matthew's Gospel, for the unusual way God works in the story that the writer is about to introduce. At first glance, the birth of Jesus appeared to be the story of a child conceived out of wedlock—and, even worse, perhaps the result of an adulterous affair. We know, of course, that this is not what happened. But the text makes clear that this troubling scenario is precisely what Joseph *thought* must have happened, when Mary came to him to explain that she was pregnant prior to their marriage.

What I love about this genealogical introduction to Matthew's Gospel, and why I don't want us to skip over it, is that most of us have been through painful experiences of our own. Some of you reading this book have lost a spouse. Some were raped. Some have known poverty that drove you to do things you never thought you would do. Some were conceived out of wedlock, and some conceived your own children out of wedlock. Matthew begins his Gospel by drawing attention to the fact that God has used just such people in the past, in all their painful and difficult circumstances, to accomplish his purposes.

This is what God does in our lives. As I look back over my life, and you look back upon yours, I think we will find that many of the best things about us may well have come from those painful experiences, redeemed by a God who, as a popular contemporary worship song notes, "makes beautiful things out of the dust."[2]

What Mary Said and What Joseph Heard

If we bring together Luke's and Matthew's accounts of Jesus' birth stories, it seems likely to me that Mary told Joseph of her pregnancy on a visit to Bethlehem, Joseph's hometown. (Luke 2:3 suggests that Bethlehem was Joseph's "own city.") Luke tells us that after Mary learned from the angel Gabriel that she was pregnant, she went to visit her older cousin Elizabeth, who was pregnant with Jesus' cousin, John the Baptist. Bethlehem was just a few miles from the hill country where Elizabeth lived, and so it seems quite possible that, after telling Elizabeth of her pregnancy, the two of them traveled to Bethlehem to explain this to Joseph. I've even wondered if Elizabeth may not have been the matchmaker who arranged for Mary's marriage to Joseph, given that she lived very close to Bethlehem but was a member of Mary's family.

Mary, likely accompanied by Elizabeth, told Joseph that a messenger from God had appeared to her announcing she was to have a child. (The Greek word that is transliterated as "angel" in the Gospels—*angelos*—literally means "messenger.") The messenger had told Mary she would become pregnant through the work of the Holy Spirit.

That may have been exactly what Mary said, but I suspect it was not exactly what Joseph heard. He seems simply to have heard that his fiancée was pregnant, and he knew he was not the father. In trying to imagine Joseph's reaction, I think back to my engagement to my wife, LaVon. We were married the week after high school graduation and had not been intimate before that. I've tried to imagine how I would have felt if, during our engagement, LaVon had told me she was pregnant by the Holy Spirit. Would I have believed her? Of course not! Neither did Joseph believe Mary.

Matthew tells us this, in so many words. We read in Matthew 1:19 that Joseph "was a righteous man," by which Matthew may have intended us to know that Joseph would not condone adultery. Matthew may also have used the phrase in reference to the next line: "Because he didn't want to humiliate her, he decided to call off their engagement quietly." Clearly Joseph did not believe Mary's story that she had conceived supernaturally by the Holy Spirit.

In a moment we'll explore what Joseph's reaction to this situation reveals about him. First, though, let's take a quick detour into Jewish marriage customs around the time of Jesus' birth.

Marriage Customs in Ancient Judaism

In Joseph's day, Jewish marriages were usually arranged by the parents, sometimes with the help of a matchmaker and often when the bride and groom were still young children. At that point, the match was more of an understanding, a nonbinding agreement. As the girl entered puberty, however, the parents' agreement turned into a formal engagement, and the marriage ceremony usually followed between one and two years after that. To cement the formal engagement, the father of the groom paid a certain sum to the father of the bride.

Joseph's father would have paid this "bride price" (called a *mohar* in Hebrew) to Mary's father. It was not a small sum. According to one commentator I have read, the *mohar* was comparable to the price of a one-bedroom house. There was a certain logic behind this custom. In a patriarchal society such as this one, the father of the bride was losing a daughter who was working in and for the family. When she married, she would become part of—and serve—another family. The bride price was compensation for the father's "loss."

A large portion of the *mohar* was set aside for the bride. It worked something like a savings account and an insurance policy. The money would go to the bride in the event her husband died prematurely or divorced her (not unlike what we call alimony and child support today). In biblical times if a woman's husband died, she could be left destitute, and hence the *mohar* was very important.

In addition to the bride price, the groom himself would also give to his bride a sum of money called the *mattan*. This, too, was hers to keep if the man died young or divorced her. Think of the *mattan* the way we think of a wedding ring today—a gift that often amounts to several months' worth of the groom's salary (at least if the groom follows the advice of jewelers!). If the husband leaves, the ring remains the property of the bride to keep or sell. That's how the *mattan* worked, too.

In addition to the *mohar* and *mattan*, the groom's family would often give expensive gifts to the bride's family. It was all part of the engagement.

At this stage in the engagement process, the parties prepared a legal document in which the groom made certain binding promises to care for his bride. In our marriage ceremonies today, both parties take vows, but in this case only the husband-to-be made promises. He would pledge to provide a house, a living, and his love. He had to make these promises publicly before at least two witnesses. This contract was (and still is) called the *ketubah*, though in Judaism today the pledges are made at the time of marriage. The *ketubah* was an important document that ensured that the husband would provide for his wife, and it stipulated that if he ever divorced her, or if he died, she was to keep the *mohar* and *mattan*, plus the gifts that had been given to her family at their engagement. This contract appears to have been the origin of the modern marriage license, but in Joseph and Mary's time it was signed at the engagement, not at the wedding ceremony. Scribes carefully prepared the *ketubah* as a legally binding document. If a husband divorced his wife and did not ensure that she was left with her *mohar* and *mattan*, a lien would be placed against his property, and everything he owned could be sold to ensure that the wife was provided for.

From studying copies of the *ketubah* that survive from the ancient world and medieval times, we can see that the wording of this legal document has remained nearly the same over the course of two thousand years. Modern Jewish couples, following the ancient tradition, have their *ketubah* beautifully stenciled and displayed in their homes.

Upon the signing of the *ketubah*, the bride and groom legally became husband and wife. They could not sleep together until after the actual wedding ceremony; but, if either of them slept with someone else during this period of time, they would be considered adulterers.[3] And that takes us back to our Scripture passage.

The Patron Saint of Doubters

I've met a lot of people who struggle with the concept of the virgin birth. For them, it seems too difficult to believe. Many of these skeptics are young adults. When I talk with them about their struggle to believe, I always remind them that they are in good company. The first person to doubt the virgin birth—or what is more accurately called the virginal conception—was Joseph.

And he was hearing about it from Mary herself! We might call Joseph the patron saint of doubters. Despite his natural doubts, he is still referred to in Matthew as a righteous man.

I also tell the questioners that neither Mark nor John in their Gospels nor Paul in his letters nor Peter in his epistles nor James or Jude mentions the virgin birth. That doesn't mean it didn't happen, but it means that in the early church a lot of people either didn't know about it, or, if they did, perhaps it wasn't as central to their faith as it was to later Christians.

I also tell doubters how I am able to make sense of the virgin birth. Some species of fish, some lizards, a variety of insects, and at least one species of snake that reproduce sexually also have been known to reproduce asexually. Scientists will likely one day clone humans. It seems a relatively minor miracle to me for the God who created the universe to provide the missing genetic information to allow Mary to conceive as a virgin.

Having said all that, it's important to remember that telling the story of the virginal conception was less about biology and more about pointing to an essential theological truth we call the Incarnation—that in Jesus, God came to us, took on flesh, and entered our humanity. That idea captured the later church's theological affirmation that Jesus was both human and divine. But Joseph understandably could not see this on the day when Mary came to say that she was pregnant and that she had not been with a man, but instead that her conception was by the Holy Spirit. If Joseph had questions about this, it's okay if you have questions too.

Joseph's Merciful Character

Returning to our story, the news that Joseph received from Mary was devastating. The *mohar* and *mattan* had been exchanged. The *ketubah* had been signed. Joseph and Mary were not yet living together as husband and wife, but Joseph undoubtedly felt utterly betrayed and humiliated. Once Mary became visibly pregnant, people were going to talk.

Joseph faced a dilemma. On the one hand, he could do what was customary in such circumstances and call off the marriage. He would have to go to the priest or into the public square and declare what had happened and why he was breaking off the engagement. To do this publicly would be to call Mary out as an adulteress. She would be publicly scorned and humiliated, as the women listed in the genealogy were. The Law of Moses (see Deuteronomy 22:20-21, 23-24) stipulates an even harsher penalty for an engaged woman who cheats on her bridegroom before they are married: "The city's elders will bring the young woman to the door of her father's house. The citizens of that city must stone her until she dies" because she had betrayed the man to whom she was engaged, her entire family, and God. "Remove such evil from your community!" says the Law.

It doesn't appear that this penalty was practiced much among Jewish people under Roman rule. But even if Mary were not put to death, she would be seen as a sinner in her community, a harlot. And she would be viewed this way from that time forward. Few men would consider marrying a woman who had cheated on her fiancé. The *mohar* and *mattan* would be returned to Joseph and his family. Mary would carry a reputation with her from then on. Her family, too, may have faced disgrace.

But that was not what Joseph wanted. Instead, even though undoubtedly heartbroken, he showed mercy to Mary. He decided to divorce her quietly. This likely meant that he would say he had changed his mind about the marriage. As it became evident that Mary was pregnant, people would assume that Joseph was the father and that he had a change of heart after being intimate with her. He, not Mary, would be seen as the dishonorable party in the relationship. He would take all the blame. He would accept the stigma and shame for himself rather than allow Mary to be forever disgraced. Mary and her family would keep the *mohar* and *mattan* as child support and alimony. Her dignity would remain intact. No one would be put to death. All this is implied by those few words in Matthew's Gospel: "Joseph her husband was a righteous man. Because he didn't want to humiliate her, he decided to call off their engagement quietly" (Matthew 1:19).

Think about the picture that Matthew's Gospel reveals of Joseph in those few words. Joseph had reason to believe that he had been wronged, that his fiancée had been unfaithful. At that point Joseph hadn't yet had the dream in which the messenger of the Lord appeared to him. Despite his pain, he still felt compassion for Mary. He showed mercy, forgiveness, and grace. He felt hurt and betrayed but refused to denounce her publicly and humiliate her. That, I think, is remarkable.

Responding to Infidelity

As I was researching and thinking about this topic, I invited friends to share with me how their lives had been affected by infidelity. Had they experienced anything like the emotional shock and pain that Joseph must have felt when he thought Mary had betrayed him? Did their marriages survive? If so, how? If not, how did they personally survive the situation?

It's a painful subject to discuss, and I am grateful to the eleven people who privately shared their stories with me. As I learned from their stories, more than half the marriages survived in spite of infidelity. Others, sadly, did not. I want to draw out a couple of things I learned in reading these stories and thinking about them in the context of Joseph's story.

Jesus stated that infidelity breaks the marriage covenant and is grounds for divorce. Paul allows the same. One is not required to stay in a marriage where there is infidelity. Joseph was not acting improperly when he planned to divorce Mary because he thought she had broken their marital covenant; as Matthew tells us, Joseph was a righteous man. His example shows us that one might divorce and still be compassionate toward one's former spouse rather than seeking to humiliate or be vengeful. Showing such compassion requires grace. I witness that grace when I see parents who make a commitment not to speak poorly about their former spouse to their children or others. And I witnessed it among the eleven injured spouses who shared their stories, because all of them showed mercy to the person who had hurt them and betrayed their trust. Some remained married and found healing for the marriage. Others did not, but all found that in showing mercy they were personally healed.

One man described his feelings to me when he learned of his wife's infidelity and pregnancy with a child that likely was not his. "This news was completely devastating," the man said. "I was lost. I couldn't focus on anything. I had panic attacks several times a day and in general didn't know what I wanted to do."

One woman who had discovered that her husband had been having an affair for the previous eighteen months wrote, "The pain was (and at times still is) unexplainably horrible.... At first I just wanted out. I wanted him as far away from me as possible."

From these stories I learned that the marriages that survived generally had the same basic factors in common:

- Most of the couples had been to church and turned to God for help. In fact, time and again people told me that learning of a spouse's infidelity had resulted in a deeper faith. One woman said, "I just wanted to weep through every service. I felt like every sermon somehow was talking to me and that God was saying, 'I've got you. It's going to be OK.'"

- They sought counseling that helped them understand what had happened and what it would take to heal the damage in their relationship if both parties were willing to try.
- They made a commitment to work on repairing the marriage, and this commitment included ending all extramarital relationships. Both parties were committed to making it work, and the one who had been unfaithful promised that the relationship that had caused such injury was over for good.
- The spouse who had the affair expressed repeated remorse and reassurance of his or her love over a long period of time for betraying the other spouse's trust.
- Finally, the injured spouses practiced forgiveness, deciding to see both their spouses and themselves as flawed human beings and not to exact retribution.

As one man wrote to me:

I looked at the one woman I had ever loved in my life and tried to decide if the affair was "enough" to take my dream girl away from me. I spent a long time searching myself for how to forgive, how to move past it and how to be happily married. In the end,

I moved past it by telling myself that everyone is human, everyone makes mistakes.... It has taken a lot of work. We still go to marriage counseling today. However, now our conversations are not about infidelity but how can we be better for our family, ourselves, and others. Looking back, I almost feel that everything that has happened has actually been a blessing and something that I cannot see myself without. It has defined me, but not in a negative way; it has defined me that through some soul searching, understanding of what forgiveness is, and hard work on myself I can get through all things.

Another person wrote, "My marriage did not survive the infidelity, but I was able to offer forgiveness. As I struggled with many emotions, I kept coming back to prayer, and in particular the prayer Jesus taught us how to pray: 'Forgive us our trespasses, as we forgive....' As is often said, forgiveness is the gift you give to yourself."

For those marriages that survived, and for those that did not, the people who practiced forgiveness and grace were eventually able to move beyond their pain and avoid living a life of bitterness and resentment.

That was what Joseph practiced even as he must have been dealing with the pain from what he believed was Mary's betrayal. When I think of three words that describe the humble carpenter in this brief passage of

Scripture, they are *merciful, gracious,* and *forgiving.* And that leads me to wonder: How many more times, as Jesus was growing up, did he see these same attributes in Joseph? How often did he watch Joseph show mercy to those who wronged him? How often was Joseph gracious to those who hurt him? How often was he the image of forgiveness?

Is it any surprise that Jesus grew to be a man who showed mercy to sinners, who taught his disciples to forgive, who called them to love their enemies, and who hung on a cross and cried out, "Father, forgive them, for they don't know what they're doing" (Luke 23:34)?

Lord, how grateful we are to you for your mercy and grace. You see the ways that we fall short, the times when we have strayed from your path, the moments when we brought pain to other people and to you. Please forgive us. Wash us clean and make us new. And help us to be, like Joseph, people who show mercy to those who have wronged us. Help us to forgive and to release our urge to seek retribution. In Jesus' name. Amen.

3

RAISING A CHILD
NOT YOUR OWN

When Mary his mother was engaged to Joseph, before they were married, she became pregnant by the Holy Spirit. Joseph her husband was a righteous man. Because he didn't want to humiliate her, he decided to call off their engagement quietly. As he was thinking about this, an angel from the Lord appeared to him in a dream and said, "Joseph son of David, don't be afraid to take Mary as your wife, because the child she carries was conceived by the Holy Spirit. She will give birth to a son, and you will call him Jesus, because he will save his people from their sins."

(Matthew 1:18-21)

3

RAISING A CHILD NOT YOUR OWN

Centuries ago there was a follower of Jesus who lived in Asia Minor—what today is Turkey. He had a heart for those in need; he was selfless and kind. According to one legend, as he approached Christmas he wanted to find a way to celebrate rightly the birth of the One who gave himself for the world. After some reflection, he settled on an idea: Find needy children in his community and do something to help them. In this he would follow the tradition of the magi, who had brought gifts to help Joseph's poor family that first Christmas. You may not know the story, but you know the name: Nicholas, who eventually became a bishop in the church and after his death was canonized as St. Nicholas.

In a time when we struggle to buy gifts for people who don't need anything, and when our children or grandchildren are often exhausted or bored by the end of Christmas, having opened so many gifts, it's important to remember the example of St. Nicholas, the inspiration behind our gift exchanges. Perhaps as we celebrate Christmas, we need to reclaim his emphasis on giving to children who are not our own, children who are most in need.

In a real way, that's what this chapter is about. Joseph chose to care for, protect, and raise a child who was not his own. In this chapter we'll look at how Joseph shaped the life and ministry of Jesus, and what that story tells us not only about this humble carpenter but about God and ourselves.

A quick recap of where we are in the story: Mary informed Joseph that, though they were engaged, she was pregnant and the child was not his. She told him that an angel had told her she was going to conceive a child by the power of the Holy Spirit, without ever having been with a man. Joseph, doubting this far-fetched explanation of Mary's pregnancy, planned quietly to call off the marriage. When he did so, others would assume he was responsible for the pregnancy and for the divorce that would follow. He would be dishonored, and Mary largely would retain her honor.

That night, after hearing Mary's news, Joseph experienced what was undoubtedly a fitful sleep. And as he slept, Joseph had a dream. In it, an angel of the Lord appeared to him, announcing that he should not be afraid to take Mary as his wife, because the child conceived in her womb was of the Holy Spirit, just as Mary had said. It is to this part of the story we now turn.

Angels

Let's begin with Matthew's account of the angel who came to Joseph in a dream. As mentioned previously, our English word *angel* is a transliteration of the Greek word *angelos*, which simply means "messenger."

We often think of angels as winged creatures, but when you read the Bible closely, that is not how they are portrayed. It is true that Scripture describes some heavenly creatures as having wings. In Isaiah 6:2, for example, Isaiah saw a group of seraphim in the temple that had six wings each. One pair of wings covered the eyes, another pair were on the feet, and the third pair were for flying. Elsewhere the Bible describes cherubim. These make us think of cherubs, with the pudgy little faces that we associate with Valentine's Day. The cherubim in the Bible have four faces. Cherubim and seraphim are not angels, but it may be from them that we get the mistaken idea that angels have wings.

Most often in the Bible, we find that angels simply look like people. Hence, the writer of Hebrews wrote to first-century Christians, "Don't neglect to open up your homes to guests, because by doing this some have been hosts to angels without knowing it" (Hebrews 13:2). The fact that we might entertain or host angels without knowing it would tell us that angels most often look like ordinary people. In the book that bears his name, Daniel speaks to the angel Gabriel and refers to him as "the man." In Luke's Gospel, when Mary speaks to Gabriel, he appears simply as a stranger, with no wings.

In Matthew's Gospel, the angel speaks to Joseph through his dreams. It happens four times. In the first dream, the angel of the Lord reveals that Mary is pregnant by the Holy Spirit and describes the child's destiny. In the second dream, an angel tells Joseph to take his family to Egypt to save the child. In the third dream, when Joseph and the Holy Family are in Egypt, he receives word from the angel of the Lord that it is safe to take his family to Mary's hometown of Nazareth. And in the fourth dream Joseph is warned not to return to Judea.

In Luke's Gospel, the angel Gabriel appears to Mary face-to-face. Why doesn't the same happen with Joseph? Why does the angel appear to Joseph only in a dream?

We can't be certain of the answer, but here's what I think. In order to see angels, I think you have to have a bit of an imagination, an openness to a different way of seeing. You have to be able to perceive something that others might not be able to see.

Did Joseph have this ability? Maybe not. Joseph was a craftsman. He worked with tools and materials to build things. Like many men, I suspect he was better at seeing how a piece of wood might become a farm implement than seeing angels in his midst. He may have said that angels were not logical. Those practical ways of thinking may impede one's ability to see angels. It seems possible that the only way God could break through to Joseph was in a dream, when Joseph's rational way of thinking was suspended. Perhaps that's why Joseph met the angel of the Lord in his dreams.

Seeing an Angel, and Being One

A woman in the congregation I serve recently told me that she and others had seen angels just after her son's death; they appeared at the gravesite. When I asked what they looked like, she said they had wings and "looked like clouds." I'll admit, the rational side of me was a bit skeptical. I asked, "Did everyone with you see the angels?" No, she said, just a few.

Another woman recently told me about her vision of angels. She and her husband had driven to St. Jude's Hospital, a place they had never visited before. She said, "I saw what looked like white sheets that were just blowing in the wind, hovering over the building." She recognized them as angels. Her husband did not see them. White sheets or angels? I don't discount that these people saw angels. I suspect that an angel might appear in whatever way someone needs them to appear in order to convey God's message.

I've never seen an angel, at least not the winged kind that flitter overhead. But once, I ran out of gas on a terribly cold and snowy day, ten miles from the nearest gas station. A guy named Jeff stopped to help. He had seen my car by the side of the road, and then he had seen me walking in the snow in the direction of a gas station. So he invited me to hop into his pickup truck. He took me to a gas station, where I bought a two-gallon gasoline can and filled it up. He waited patiently and then took me back to my car. I got out my billfold and was going to give him fifty dollars for stopping to help, but he refused. He said, "This was a blessing for me. If you give me money, you'll rob me of the blessing." So I thanked him profusely, and he drove away. I've never seen him again.

Sometimes when I think of angels, I think of Jeff. Perhaps God sent Jeff as his way of looking out for me. Most often the angels God sends today have names such as yours. These angels come to offer a word of encouragement or guidance, or to offer a bit of tangible help. Sometimes, like Joseph's angel, they help us know God's will and then help us find the courage to do it.

Recently, one of our church members told me about her experience with angels. She and her husband were in a terrible car accident more than twenty years ago, an accident that would claim his life. She was able to get out of the vehicle, but her husband was trapped inside the car. While she stood there crying, waiting for help, a car carrying three teenage girls stopped. The girls stood by her side for an hour as the police tried to extricate her husband from the vehicle. He died on the scene. But she told me she would never forget how those three teenage girls who had never met her before simply stood with her at the side of the road through the terrible ordeal.

I wonder, have you ever met this kind of angel? Or maybe, more importantly, have you ever been one of these angels for someone else, perhaps a complete stranger who was in need? Maybe you saw someone who had run out of gas or who had been in an accident. Maybe you met someone who needed a word of encouragement, so you offered it. Maybe God used you as an angel without your even realizing it.

Those of you reading this book during Advent may know that the third Sunday in Advent is traditionally known as Gaudete Sunday. *Gaudete* is the Latin word for "rejoice," and the Sunday of this week is known as Joy Sunday. Those using Advent candle wreaths may recognize that the color for this week's candle is pink, a symbol of joy. This weekend foreshadows the joy Christians sing about on Christmas Eve or Christmas morning as they join together in Isaac Watts's famous carol "Joy to the World."

Sadly, the season leading up to Christmas is often anything but joyful. We may sing of joy, but we don't necessarily feel it. Beyond all the chaos of our preparations for Christmas, all the tasks to be done in a finite amount of time, what often makes this season feel so joyless is this: In our minds we have an idealized picture of Christmas, and it doesn't always match our real-life experience. Life for us doesn't look like a Norman Rockwell painting. (The first Christmas didn't look like a Norman Rockwell painting either.) In fact, depending on what's happening in our lives at the time, Christmas can be really depressing.

So, where do we look for joy during Advent and Christmas when it seems to be missing in our lives? We can find it in being an angel for someone else. We experience joy when we take our eyes off our own situation and focus on blessing, building up, encouraging, or serving others. After Jeff helped me on that snowy day when I ran out of gas, I felt deeply grateful. But in stopping to help me, I'm pretty sure Jeff felt real joy. When we take our eyes off ourselves and focus on someone else, we open ourselves to a different way of seeing and being. We become someone's angel, a messenger of God's good news, a gift during a time of need.

When was the last time you were someone's angel?

Completing the Story

Any Jew who heard Matthew's account of Joseph's dreams instantly would have thought of another Joseph in Scripture—the favorite son of Jacob (Israel), who lived at least sixteen hundred years before the birth of Jesus. If you've not read his story in Genesis you may have seen a version of it on stage in *Joseph and the Amazing Technicolor Dreamcoat*. You'll remember that the earlier Joseph was also a man who heard from God in his dreams. Matthew often draws parallels between the life of Jesus and stories and figures from the Old

Testament, and it seems likely he intended for us to see that earlier Joseph as a kind of type or picture of how God was at work in the dreams of Joseph the carpenter.

Frequently Matthew quotes Old Testament Scripture, using words such as these: "Now all of this took place so that what the Lord had spoken through the prophet would be fulfilled..." (Matthew 1:22). Sometimes we mistakenly read Matthew's words to mean that the Old Testament texts quoted were predictive prophesies being fulfilled in Jesus. The Greek word for *fulfilled* also means "completed," and it is this sense of the word that Matthew wants us to understand. He and other New Testament authors clearly saw Jesus as completing the prophets' words, or bringing a new and deeper fulfillment of them. Jesus represented a fuller, more complete expression of the Old Testament story—a story of God rescuing his people and showing them how to live in harmony with God and one another.*

---

* Scholars note that among the important ways in which Matthew portrays Jesus, he points to Jesus as one like, but greater than, Moses. For example, there are five sections in Matthew's Gospel, corresponding to the five books of Moses. And just as Moses received the Law and brought it to the people from a mountain, Matthew shows Jesus delivering God's new law from a mountain (in the Sermon on the Mount). At one point in Matthew, Jesus even goes onto a mountain and meets with Moses (and Elijah). There are many other parallels as well.

In addition, Matthew wants us to see that Joseph, the earthly father of Jesus, heard from God in dreams—just as Joseph, the Old Testament patriarch, heard from God in dreams. To make the parallel even stronger, just as the father of Joseph the patriarch was named Jacob, so Matthew notes that the father of Joseph the carpenter was named Jacob (Matthew 1:16).

Don't Be Afraid

Returning to the dream of Joseph the carpenter, we read that the angel told him:

> *"Joseph son of David, don't be afraid to take*
> *Mary as your wife, because the child she carries*
> *was conceived by the Holy Spirit. She will give*
> *birth to a son, and you will call him Jesus,*
> *because he will save his people from their sins."*
> *(Matthew 1:20-21)*

I find it interesting that, after calling Joseph's name, the first words the angel speaks to Joseph are "Don't be afraid." Imagine that as a conversation starter!

I think about the times when I'm talking with my wife, LaVon, and the first thing I tell her is, "Don't be mad, but...." It's a cue that whatever I tell her next will give her good reason to be mad.

Joseph probably got that same feeling of apprehension when the angel began with "Don't be afraid." When God calls you to do something and the opening words are "Don't be afraid," you likely *should* be afraid! Whatever follows is sure to be outside your comfort zone. It may be a call filled with challenge and risk. In fact, sometimes God will call us to do the thing we absolutely do not want to do.

I've never seen an angel in a dream, but other kinds of angels have occasionally called me to do things I really didn't want to do.

Nancy Brown is one of those angels. She is a dynamo of a woman, twenty-three years my senior, who nearly broke my arm twisting it. Nancy told me that I needed to go with her to Africa to see what God was doing through the Methodist churches there. She hoped that if I saw it with my own eyes, I'd be as moved as she was and would come back to the States willing to do all I could to support God's work in Malawi, Zambia, and South Africa.

I'm not sure I was afraid, but I certainly dreaded the twenty-two hours of airplane rides and four hours of bus rides to reach a place I'd never been before, meeting people I'd never met and eating food I'd never eaten. But by the time we had finished, after seeing what could be done in partnership and hearing an invitation to serve with our new friends, I came back to the United States deeply inspired. I've had the satisfaction of returning to Africa several times since. The angels that call me to do things I don't want to do, things that I may dread, things that I end up doing joyfully—those angels usually look a lot like Nancy Brown and others in the congregation I serve.

Why did the angel tell Joseph not to be afraid? It wasn't that Joseph might fear the angel itself. The message really was this: "Don't be afraid of this mission to take Mary as your wife and to raise this child as your own." The challenge of doing so must have made this humble carpenter anxious or fearful. He was being given a mission to wed Mary and to trust that the child was of God and not of another man. But more than that, Joseph was being presented with a mission of raising this child who "will save his people from their sins." Don't be afraid, Joseph. God's saving plans for the world are being entrusted to your care!

"Don't be afraid" is one of the most often recorded statements by God in the Bible. That God so frequently has to tell us not to be afraid is, once again, a reminder that God's calling is not for the faint of heart.

God called Moses back to Egypt to confront Pharaoh and demand that he release the Israelite slaves. You may recall the reaction of Moses, who was eighty years old at the time. He said, basically, "Are you kidding me?" (His actual words were "Please send someone else!")

We are a bit like Moses. It's our nature to make excuses and raise objections when called to do something we don't want to do. But what God called Moses to wasn't just any task; it was saving an entire nation.

Likewise, what God asked of Joseph was no ordinary or small thing: he was to raise, protect, and nurture God's son, so that the Messiah could grow up and save his people. It was as if the entirety of Moses' life, and Joseph's, had been preparing them for this moment, when God would call them to play a key part in God's saving story. Yes, it was scary. It was downright terrifying. And yet it was a mission that would change the world.

Have you ever felt God calling you to do something that scared you just a little bit? If not, perhaps you haven't been paying attention. If you have heard God's call and responded with a leap of faith that took you beyond your comfort zone, then you've probably discovered something important: Trusting God despite our fears, saying yes to God's call even when we feel like saying no, ultimately brings us joy. It's the kind of joy we celebrate on Joy Sunday in Advent.

I know a woman whose initial reaction to anything uncomfortable or unnerving is to say no. It's a kind of default response that comes from fear. She tends to see all the things that could go wrong, or all the ways she isn't equipped or the right person for the job. One thing I admire about her, though, is that her initial response is usually not her final response. The Holy Spirit continues to work on her, and eventually her fear gives way to faith, her no becomes a yes, and God uses her to do amazing things.

We all have a thousand excellent excuses to avoid what God is calling us to do, but it's in saying yes that life's adventures are found! I think of those who tutor kids in low-income neighborhoods where they've never been before. And those who decide to start giving 10 percent or more of their income, who worry at first but then enter into a lifestyle of trust and extravagant giving. And those in our congregation who have answered the call to ordained ministry. And those who volunteer in prison ministry. And all those who, in some form or another, give a hesitant yes when they want to say no. There's a bit of anxiety in each of these cases.

For me, there was more than a bit of anxiety when I received a phone call in 1990 with word that Bishop W. T. Handy was assigning me to start a new church for people who didn't go to church. He said the assignment involved just a few problems: There was no land and no place for the congregation to meet, there was no money, and there were no people. I was excited, and at the same time I was terrified.

God says over and over in Scripture, in essence: "Don't be afraid! Don't surrender to your fears! I've got something important for you to do. And I'm going to do something great, if only you will put one foot in front of the other."

Every great thing you'll ever be called by God to do will require an element of risk. It will require you to take a leap of faith. It will require you to do something that involves uncertainty, and all you'll have to lean on is the faith that God has called you. These ventures will require you to become vulnerable and to risk getting it wrong, falling flat on your face, making a fool of yourself, or being made the fool by someone else. And yet: "Don't be afraid," the angel of the Lord said to Joseph in that dream.

When was the last time you felt God calling you to do something that made you anxious or afraid? When was the last time you said yes to that call when you really felt like saying no?

On Joy Sunday or any other day, my hope is that you will remind yourself that almost all your most exciting, life-giving, and joy-filled experiences have come because you took a risk, stepped outside your comfort zone, and said yes to God's call in spite of your fears. Remember what the angel told Joseph: "Joseph son of David, don't be afraid to take Mary as your wife, because the child she carries was conceived by the Holy Spirit. She will give birth to a son, and you will call him Jesus, because he will save his people from their sins."

Raising a Child Not Your Own

One of the most challenging and frightening parts of Joseph's call was the enormous task that God entrusted to Joseph. The messenger of God told him that the child Mary was carrying would be very important indeed: he would be the savior of his people, and Joseph would assume responsibility for him. Some call Joseph an adoptive father, because for all intents and purposes he did adopt and raise Jesus as his own. Some see him as a stepfather, since he was Jesus' father by marriage. Some might even call him a foster father.

The mission given to Joseph was to raise this boy as though he were Joseph's own. It was to love him, mentor him, teach him, and guide him. It was to model for this child what it meant to be a man—a man who honored and served God. Jesus was not Joseph's child by birth, but the boy would need Joseph to love him as his own.

Listen carefully: God's plan for the redemption of the world depended on one man's willingness to raise a child who was not his own.

There are stepparents and adoptive parents and foster parents who understand this role as a mission; they know from the beginning that it will be hard work. They take on a call that can be frightening. And to them, too, God says, "Don't be afraid."

As I was working on this book, I spoke with a member of our church staff, Frank Gentile, one of the greatest people I've ever known, about his experience of becoming a stepfather. His comments capture dimensions of the mission that Joseph was taking on. Frank helped me see Jesus' earthly father with fresh eyes.

> I met my wife Yvonne on vacation. I went out on a date with her. She had two children from a previous marriage. And so for us it was not just dating, getting to know each other personally. I was also getting to know the kids. When you're in a relationship with somebody that's just single, it's really all about you and that individual. But when you're thrust into a situation where there are kids present already, a lot of things hit your mind. One of my fears was: Would I be seen by the children as a father figure or not? Would we be just kind of friends? The words that any stepfather dreads are, "Well, you're not my father."

As we progressed toward marriage I explained to the kids that it had to be a package deal. It couldn't be just about my relationship with their mom; it had to be about the kids as well. I think about what Joseph must have gone through. You know, that's not his natural-born child, but that kid still needs a father. I think that feeling of responsibility sometimes could be such a weight. It's like you and that kid against the world. And you feel that you've been endowed with a certain sense of "I've gotta be the one who helps this person get through life. And on the way I've gotta figure it out for myself, too." When I think about my own kids, I hope that I'm passing on to them a love for other people, and that that's one of the highest callings that you could have.

Many of you reading this book are stepmoms or stepdads. Some of you are adoptive mothers or adoptive fathers. Some have served as foster parents. Yours is a challenging but high calling. Sometimes it is hard. Sometimes you give of yourself but the love is not reciprocated. I have described Joseph as the patron saint of doubters. I would suggest that he is also the patron saint of foster parents, stepparents, and adoptive parents.

Perhaps nowhere is the selfless, sacrificial love of God more clearly displayed than when someone takes on the task of raising and loving a child who is not biologically theirs. They didn't have to take the job, they had a choice, but they chose to set aside their fears and accept the calling to be a stepparent, foster parent, or adoptive parent.

I have a stepmom, and I had a stepdad until his death a couple of years ago. I know that being a stepparent is a hard gig. You take on the role of being a parent for someone who doesn't necessarily want to see you in that role. Sometimes, kids hold on to a dream that, one day, their mom and dad will marry again. As a stepparent, you stand in the way of that dream becoming reality. It's hard enough to get along with your parents during your teenage years; it's even harder when you're dealing with someone who's not biologically your parent. It can create great conflict, and it can mean that the stepparent or foster parent ends up absorbing injury and pain. In a way, that's the job that Joseph signed up for.

In his epistle, James writes these well-known words: "Religion that is pure and undefiled before God, the Father, is this: to care for orphans and widows in their distress" (James 1:27 NRSV). In the first century, widows, divorced women, and single mothers, along with their children and the children who had no parents, were the most vulnerable members of society. Again and again the Scriptures call us to care for widows and orphans. Jesus wasn't an orphan, but he did need an earthly father.

At the Church of the Resurrection, we have a ministry called A Child's Hope. It focuses on foster and adoptive care: raising up, training, and supporting people who open their homes to foster children, and supporting those who are contemplating adoption. There are currently over four hundred thousand children in the U.S. who are in the foster system at any one time.[1] Not every foster home is a loving and caring environment, though many are.

For the most part, foster children are not babies, because babies are the ones for whom it's easiest to find permanent adoptive homes. Foster kids are older. Some are in high school. When they don't have a loving family environment and they "age out" of the system, many will struggle. One survey suggests that almost 37 percent of foster kids who aged out of the system have experienced some form of homelessness.[2] But when loving foster parents step up, they can have a huge impact. In the process, they are following the example that Joseph set.

In a similar way, those adopting children can have an impact that is nearly incalculable. Adoption is not an easy path. There can be challenges and at times pain. But adopting a child who needs a family can change the world for that young person. I've watched dozens of families heroically raise and care for adopted children. At times it's quite difficult. But the trajectory of these kids' lives is forever changed because of sacrifices made and love given by their adoptive parents.

Not all of us are in a position to become foster or adoptive parents. All of us, though, are called to act in the spirit of Joseph and help care for and build up children who are not our own.

When you think about it, we all perform this work in our own particular ways. Some teach Sunday school, passing along spiritual values to the children of others. Some coach. Some volunteer as tutors, Big Brothers, or Big Sisters. These roles can be critical, because when children reach their middle school or high school years, they don't always listen to their parents' views. Sometimes the only person who can break through to them is a Sunday school teacher or youth group mentor, a Scout leader or coach on their sports team. There are millions of children who need caring adults to mentor them, listen to them, and offer them positive role models. All of us are called. Each of us can make a difference.

Christmas takes on real significance when we move beyond buying gifts for people who don't need anything to becoming modern-day Josephs and looking for ways to care for children who need our support.

At Church of the Resurrection, the Christmas Eve candlelight service is the best-attended worship service each year. Following the lead of Ginghamsburg Church in Ohio, some years ago we began giving away the entire Christmas Eve offering to projects benefiting children in poverty. Half goes to support projects in developing countries, many of which are focused on orphans; the other half stays in the Kansas City area and is focused on improving the quality of life for low-income children. We do more than give money. We look at ways we can give our time to invest in these children, both in our city and abroad.

Mike Slaughter, pastor emeritus at Ginghamsburg, regularly reminds his congregation, "Christmas is not your birthday." Maybe that's a lesson we need to learn for ourselves and teach our kids. We spend a lot of time and money buying things for people who don't really need them. But we celebrate Christmas in the right spirit when we care for children in need, just as St. Nicholas did, just as the wise men did, and just as Joseph did when he looked past his fear, took Mary as his wife, and raised Jesus as his own son.

Lord, how grateful we are for Joseph's story. Please help us hear your call on our lives and become the instruments through which you bless others. Help us not to be afraid when you call us to do something that calls for a risk or challenge. Give us the courage to step outside our comfort zone and take a leap of faith. Finally, Lord, help us to feel responsible for children who are not our own and to experience the joy that comes in helping them. In Jesus' name. Amen.

4

THE JOURNEY TO BETHLEHEM

In those days Caesar Augustus declared that everyone throughout the empire should be enrolled in the tax lists. This first enrollment occurred when Quirinius governed Syria. Everyone went to their own cities to be enrolled. Since Joseph belonged to David's house and family line, he went up from the city of Nazareth in Galilee to David's city, called Bethlehem, in Judea. He went to be enrolled together with Mary, who was promised to him in marriage and who was pregnant.

(Luke 2:1-5)

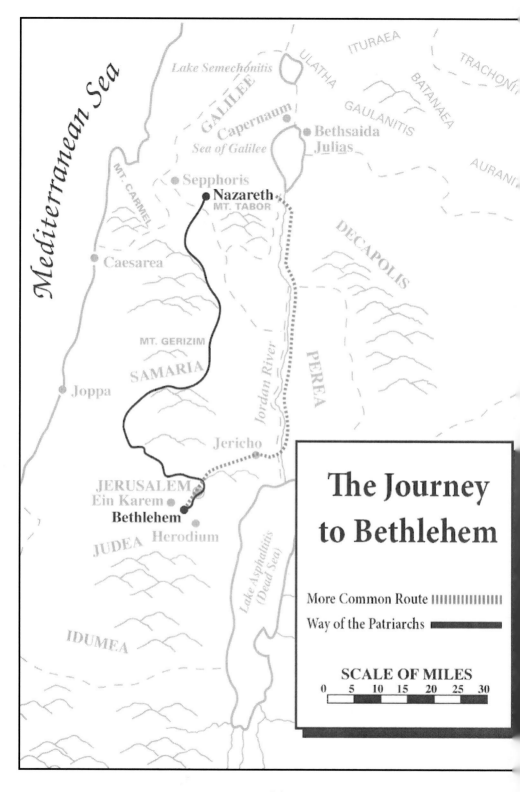

Mediterranean Sea

Lake Semechonitis

ITURAEA

TRACHONIT

ULATHA

GALILEE

BATANAEA

GAULANITIS

Capernaum

Bethsaida
Julias

Sea of Galilee

AURANI

Sepphoris

Nazareth
MT. TABOR

DECAPOLIS

Caesarea

MT. CARMEL

MT. GERIZIM

SAMARIA

Jordan River

PEREA

Joppa

Jericho

JERUSALEM
Ein Karem
Bethlehem

Herodium

Lake Asphaltitis
(Dead Sea)

JUDEA

IDUMEA

The Journey
to Bethlehem

More Common Route |||||||||||||||||

Way of the Patriarchs ▬▬▬▬

SCALE OF MILES

0   5   10   15   20   25   30

4

THE JOURNEY TO BETHLEHEM

Up to this point in Joseph's story we've looked primarily to the Gospel of Matthew. We'll return to Matthew in the next chapter, but before doing that let's turn to Luke's account of the stories surrounding Jesus' birth.

It might be helpful at this point to note that Matthew and Luke wrote their Gospels independent of one another. However, they apparently shared a couple of common sources, and hence they tell the story of Jesus in much the same way.* But they also each drew from sources the other did not have, and so there are

---

* Both Matthew and Luke seem to have had an early version of Mark's Gospel, as well as another source that scholars call Q—from the German word *Quelle*, meaning "source"—which appears to have contained many of Jesus' sayings.

differences between the two Gospels. We see those differences particularly in the stories surrounding Jesus' birth.

If we were to cut, copy, and paste the Christmas stories from both Gospels side by side, we would find that they agree at many points. They agree that Jesus' parents' names were Joseph and Mary, that Jesus was born in Bethlehem, that Mary was a virgin when she conceived Jesus by the Holy Spirit, and that Jesus ultimately was raised in Nazareth, not Bethlehem.

But you might also be surprised at how much the Christmas stories differ from each other. If we had only Luke's Gospel, we would assume that both Joseph and Mary lived in Nazareth; if we only had Matthew's Gospel we might assume they lived in Bethlehem. If we only had Luke's Gospel we would assume that Mary gave birth in a stable; if we only had Matthew's Gospel we would think she gave birth in Joseph's family home. If we only had Luke's Gospel we would think that six weeks after Jesus' birth the Holy Family returned to Nazareth; if we only had Matthew's Gospel we would assume the Holy Family lived as refugees in Egypt for months, perhaps years, before Herod finally died, and that they only moved to Nazareth because Joseph was warned in a dream not to return to Judea. There are many other differences in Matthew and Luke's Nativity accounts.

Some of these differences can easily be harmonized or reconciled with one another, while others are a bit more difficult to fit together.

Before we consider the arduous journey that Joseph and Mary made from Nazareth to Bethlehem just before Jesus' birth, I'd like to show you on a map where various parts of Matthew's and Luke's accounts of the Nativity took place.

A Lesson in Biblical Geography and History

Let's begin by clarifying where and when the various events in this story took place, as this helps us understand the events we remember year after year at Christmas.

Take a look at the map at the beginning of this chapter and notice the proximity of the places mentioned in the Nativity stories: Luke is clear that Mary's hometown is Nazareth, in the Galilee region of the Holy Land. Matthew implies (and many scholars believe Luke does as well) that Joseph's hometown was Bethlehem, seventy miles south of Nazareth as the crow flies and about five miles southwest of Jerusalem. Mary's elder cousin Elizabeth, to whom Mary makes a visit following the Annunciation, lived with her husband Zechariah in the "hill country of Judea" (Luke 1:65 NRSV), and tradition says the place was Ein Karem, a few miles west of Jerusalem and north of Bethlehem. Thus, Joseph and Elizabeth lived relatively close by. Mary's home was some distance away, across the mountains that divide the Holy Land.

That's the "where" of the story; now for the "when." It can be difficult to harmonize the events described in Matthew's and Luke's accounts of the Nativity story. On the opposite page I offer for your consideration one possible sequence of events from those two accounts.

A Hastily Arranged Wedding

It is not uncommon for me to officiate at weddings where the wife is pregnant or the couple already have children together before getting married. But in biblical times, if a woman was found to be pregnant by her fiancé (frowned upon then but not entirely uncommon) the marriage ceremony was unlikely to be postponed. We learn in Matthew that after Mary told Joseph of her pregnancy, he was visited by an angel as he slept, commanding him to wed Mary. Matthew then tells us: "When Joseph woke up, he did just as an angel from God commanded and took Mary as his wife" (Matthew 1:24).

In modern times, there used to be more shame associated with a wedding where the bride was expecting a child. The custom was that the bride's wedding dress

Events in
the Nativity Story

Elizabeth, Mary's kin, conceives John the Baptist.

Six months after Elizabeth conceives, Mary learns she will have a child.

Mary immediately travels to Elizabeth's home to tell her she's pregnant.

Mary (with Elizabeth?) travels to Bethlehem to give Joseph the news.

Joseph decides to break off the engagement.

That night, Joseph has a dream in which he is told to wed Mary.

Joseph and Mary formally marry shortly after his dream.

Joseph and Mary settle in Nazareth, Mary's hometown.

In the eighth or ninth month, an imperial census is called.

Joseph and Mary travel back to Bethlehem.

Mary gives birth in the stable using a manger as a crib for Jesus.

Shepherds, beckoned by the angels, arrive to see Jesus.

Joseph and Mary move into the guest room of Joseph's family home.

Eight days after his birth, Jesus is circumcised.

Forty days after his birth, he is presented in the temple.

Forty-one days to eighteen months after Jesus' birth, the magi arrive.

Herod orders the death of the boy children of Bethlehem.

Joseph and Mary flee to Egypt, where they remain until Herod's death.

Joseph and Mary return and settle in Nazareth.

would not be white; wearing a different color was a kind of public sign that the couple had not waited until their wedding night to be intimate. When I was first ordained this was still common practice. Meeting with couples who were expediting their wedding, I would remind them that Mary and Joseph's wedding was expedited because she, too, was expecting when she married.

It is possible that Joseph married Mary in Bethlehem. Typically after a couple married, the woman moved in with her husband, often in a new addition to his parents' home. It is still the case in many communities in the Middle East. I have been in the homes of Palestinian Christians who, after marrying, added another floor onto their parents' home for their own "flat." If Joseph was from Bethlehem, we would expect the couple would live there.

But Luke tells us that they were in Nazareth at the time when Augustus demanded a census be taken. This might tell us that Joseph took Mary to Nazareth after determining that he would not call off the marriage. It is customary today that when the bride and groom are from different hometowns, the wedding takes place in the bride's community, and, if she grew up going to church, in her home church. In the same way we might expect that Joseph and Mary's wedding may have taken place in Nazareth.

Do you think Joseph and Mary sought to explain to their family and friends about the visit of the angels and Mary's supernatural conception? Joseph didn't believe it without an angel appearing to him in a dream. Would others believe it? We know Mary told Elizabeth and Zechariah, her older kin, and they believed her. But I suspect that neither Joseph nor Mary told many others about this. Later in the Gospels, when visiting his hometown Nazareth, Jesus was referred to as Joseph's son. I suspect that since the wedding was expedited, Joseph simply accepted the snickers and whispers behind his back as family and friends alike assumed he'd taken advantage of Mary prior to the wedding.

Following the wedding, rather than returning to Bethlehem, Joseph and Mary remained in Nazareth. Was this Joseph's way of ensuring that Mary was surrounded by friends and family through her pregnancy? We don't know. What we do know, according to Luke, is that the couple were living in Nazareth when the emperor called for a census, just weeks before Mary was to give birth.

The Enrollment/Census

Luke tells us, "In those days Caesar Augustus declared that everyone throughout the empire should be enrolled in the tax lists. This first enrollment occurred when Quirinius governed Syria." (Luke 2:1-2). At regular intervals the Roman government conducted a census in various parts of the empire. In ancient Rome it happened every five years. By the time of Augustus the census was only once every fourteen years.* Augustus conducted a census three times during his long reign. One individual was appointed to oversee the entire census, and local people were assigned to go to each village and make the counts.

In the United States, our census aims to get an accurate count of the population and basic demographic data that are used for many purposes. We also have officials who assess taxes on our property, completely unrelated to the census. Finally, the US Congress sets the tax rates and the Internal Revenue Service enforces the tax code, ensuring we pay our income taxes. These three different functions—statistics, property tax assessment, and income tax assessment—were all combined in the Roman census. The Romans wanted to register each person in the empire and ascertain how much property each possessed, in order to determine the taxes to be collected across the empire.

---

* There are historical challenges with the timing of this census: Quirinius was not governor of Syria until AD 6, while King Herod, ruler of Judea, died in 4 BC. Some have speculated that Quirinius took a census in this region while serving in another role in Syria and did so just before Herod died—hence Luke's mention that this was the "first" census taken while Quirinius held an administrative position in Syria.

Once the Romans obtained an accurate census of a town or village, they would determine how much tax that village would have to pay. Some people in the town would bid on the opportunity to become the tax collector, whose job was to collect from neighbors the amount required by the Romans plus the tax collector's share. Whatever the tax collectors took in beyond the required amount of tax was theirs to keep as salary. (You can begin to see why tax collectors in Jesus' day were so hated.)

The penalties for failure to appear for the census were serious. Senators who violated this requirement were removed from the senate. Men of the equestrian class lost their horses. But for the ordinary subjects of Rome such as Joseph, who were not citizens, the penalty was much more severe: imprisonment, confiscation of property, scourging, or slavery.[1] This is why there was urgency for Joseph to return to his hometown. He had no choice but to go back to Bethlehem and comply.

Typically, only the man needed to appear before the census-taker. Why then did Joseph take the very pregnant Mary on the long journey to Bethlehem if it was not required by Roman law? We can't know for sure, but we do know that the census tended to foster rebellion among the Jews. Acts 5:37 mentions one revolt that occurred during Jesus' lifetime as a result of a census. And shortly after the birth of Jesus an armed rebellion took place just a few miles from Nazareth, in Sepphoris. The Roman army descended upon the region, killing many and taking others away as slaves.

I believe Joseph took Mary with him to Bethlehem for fear that, in the troubled times of a census, something might happen to her and the child she was carrying if she remained in Nazareth. I think he took Mary to protect her, not wanting her to be out of his sight during a time of potential danger.

But I also see the Spirit's work in nudging Joseph to take Mary with him to Bethlehem. Why would God nudge Joseph to take Mary on this difficult journey just before she gave birth? I believe that God intended that Jesus be born in Bethlehem.

Writing seven hundred years before the birth of Jesus, Micah foretold that a future king of Israel would come from Bethlehem, where King David had been born, and would reign forever:

> *As for you, Bethlehem of Ephrathah,*
> *though you are the least significant of*
> *Judah's forces,*
> *one who is to be a ruler in Israel on*
> *my behalf will come out from you.*

*His origin is from remote times, from
ancient days.*

(Micah 5:2)

Joseph and Mary could not know that magi from
Persia would be coming to Bethlehem, based upon this
text from Micah, looking for a child who was born "king
of the Jews." All Joseph knew was that something inside
was telling him he needed to take Mary with him as he
returned to his hometown to be registered.

It's interesting how God works in our lives. If we pay
attention we'll often feel the nudge of the Holy Spirit
guiding us, just as I suspect Joseph felt. As we pay
attention, listen, and act accordingly, we find ourselves
in the midst of something God is doing to accomplish
his purposes in our lives. We speak of this as God's
providence. Joseph and Mary were undoubtedly upset
by the census and the need to travel for nine days to
Bethlehem just before Mary would give birth. But God
took the emperor's decree for a census, nudged Joseph
to take Mary with him to Bethlehem, and caused Jesus'
humble birth to take place in Bethlehem, the very place
the magi would go to find him.

Over time, I've come to trust in God's providence—
that God works even through adverse circumstances, if I

only pay attention. I look back on my own life and see this in large ways and small. Following my parents' divorce, my mother remarried when I was twelve and our family moved. At the time of the divorce, our move seemed to me like the worst thing that could have happened in my life. Now, I don't believe that God willed my parents to divorce, but I do see God working through these circumstances. Many of the most important things in my life happened as a result of the divorce, remarriage, and move. I came to faith; I met my future wife; I heard a call to ordained ministry, all in the years following that move. What at the time was a terribly painful moment led to so many gifts and blessings in my life. I could not see it when I was twelve. But now at fifty-three I count on the fact that God doesn't cause painful things, but he brings good from them and works in and through them, if we're only paying attention.

The Journey

So, Joseph and a very pregnant Mary set out from Nazareth to Bethlehem. There were two routes they could have chosen, which you can see on the map on page 86. Many Jews traveling from Galilee to Judea would travel southeast, to the Jordan River Valley, crossing the Jordan or staying near it, skirting or bypassing Samaria.

This was the more common route, because relations between Jews and Samaritans were not good.*

Another possible route followed an ancient roadway known as the Way of the Patriarchs. This route cut right through the heart of Samaria. It was the shortest route, though it not only included passing through sometimes hostile territory, but also involved traversing the hills and finally the mountains that divide the Holy Land.

We can't know for certain which path Mary and Joseph took, but my guess is that Joseph took the route through the region of the Samaritans. Why this way and not the other? Again, we have to read between the lines. Jesus regularly ministered with Samaritans, passed through Samaria, and made Samaritans the heroes of his parables, singling them out for affirmation as he ministered with the multitudes. I believe it's likely that his heart for the Samaritans, who were often treated poorly by the Jews, came from Joseph, who himself knew what it was like to be treated as "less than." If Joseph did in fact influence Jesus' concern for the Samaritans, then it seems unlikely to me that he would have avoided taking the shorter route through Samaria to Bethlehem.

---

* It's interesting that the region of Samaria in the first century was roughly the same as the West Bank territories of the Palestinians today. And the relationship between Jews and Samaritans in the first century was not dissimilar to the relationship between Jews and Palestinians today.

Several years ago I retraced the steps of Joseph and Mary on their trip to Bethlehem in another book, *The Journey*. We followed the Way of the Patriarchs. Though we drove most of it, at points I would walk the route just to get a sense of what Joseph and Mary may have seen and experienced. We stopped at ancient springs where travelers drew water while making the journey.

We often picture Mary on a donkey during this seventy-mile trip. Though Scripture doesn't specifically mention a donkey, we can assume that Joseph would have procured a donkey for the pregnant Mary. Many commentators suggest the journey took three days, and that might be true if you simply calculate how many miles one might walk in a day. But this journey likely took much longer. There were hills and mountains to climb. Each day's travel needed to end at a water source for the animals. And Mary was very pregnant. Several years ago a BBC journalist procured a donkey and walked the route. It took him nine days.[2]

The Journeys We Don't Want to Take

Walking the hills and mountains of the route to Bethlehem, I found myself winded and wondered what the trip might have been like for a young pregnant woman in the eighth or ninth month of her pregnancy.

As it happened, as I was working on this book one of the associate pastors I serve with, Katherine Ebling Frazier, was nine months pregnant. I met with Katherine and her husband, Andy Frazier, also a United Methodist pastor, and asked them to imagine taking this journey. Here are a few of Kathrine's reflections about what Mary may have been feeling on that journey:

- "At this point, pregnancy feels very exhausting. I have body aches and nausea and I can't sleep. There's just a whole lot of buildup in this time. This is an exciting thing. It's unlike anything I've felt before, but it's stressful."

- "Right now I dread riding in a car for longer than thirty minutes. So there's no way Andy would be getting me on a donkey! That's not happening."

- "When you look at all the art that shows Mary on the journey, riding her donkey, she's sitting side-saddle and smiling. I would imagine her weeping and at moments screaming at Joseph. Maybe she's a little moody. I don't quite imagine it would be so delightful as the pictures portray it."

- "I think I'm terrified in a lot of ways. I wonder if Mary felt some of that as well."

From these snippets you can imagine the anxiety Mary and Joseph must have been feeling. This journey from Nazareth to Bethlehem surely was uncomfortable, unpleasant, and frightening. In Mary's time, women died in childbirth with a frequency that led to an average life expectancy of only thirty-five. The trip Joseph and Mary were making was filled with frightening possibilities.

They set out for Bethlehem reminded once more that they were living under Roman occupation. I suspect Mary left in tears, saying goodbye to her family and hometown at the moment she needed them the most. This was a journey that neither Mary nor Joseph wanted to take. It was forced upon them.

The situation that Mary and Joseph faced is emblematic of what often happens in life. At times, all of us find ourselves on journeys we don't want to take. Sometimes, as with Mary and Joseph, the journeys happen because of someone else's decisions or actions (in this case, it was the emperor). The journeys may be painful, and we may find ourselves brokenhearted or deeply discouraged along the way. We might even think that God is punishing us or has abandoned us. But God promises to sustain us, even though we may walk through the darkest valleys. God tells us to turn our burdens over to him, and he can make something beautiful of them.

Throughout Scripture we see journeys that people don't want to take, and much of the Bible is about God using and working through those journeys. There's Noah on his ark, and Abraham and Sarah uprooted in retirement and sent by God to the Promised Land. There's Ruth and Naomi grieving the loss of their husbands, and Daniel thrown into the lions' den.

Most of the really remarkable people I have met, people who are having an impact on the world, have been on journeys they didn't want to take.

Have you ever been forced on a journey you didn't want to take? It may have been your parents' divorce, or your own. Maybe it was an illness or a move or the loss of a job. Maybe it was the death of someone you loved dearly. I'm not suggesting that God caused these things to happen or that they were God's will. They are simply part of life. But God goes with you on these journeys, and God's providence has a way of bringing good and beautiful things from the pain, heartache, and disappointments we face in life. That's what Mary and Joseph discovered.

Did you know that nearly half of Luke's Gospel is devoted to telling the story of Jesus' final journey to Jerusalem, where he would be crucified? Where did Jesus learn to walk the journeys he did not want to take, trusting that God was with him? Perhaps it was from hearing Joseph talk about the difficult journey he and Mary took in faith and about what God brought forth from it. Just as Joseph had known somehow that God was with him, Jesus on his final journey knew somehow that God would redeem his suffering and use it to transform the world.

All of us go on journeys we don't want to take. In the midst of them, if we open ourselves to God, we can see God's hand leading us. When you find yourself on an unplanned and difficult journey, recall these words from the prophet Isaiah, who was writing to encourage the Jewish people during their own difficult journey in exile:

> *The LORD is the everlasting God,*
> *the creator of the ends of the earth.*
> *He doesn't grow tired or weary.*
> *His understanding is beyond human reach,*
> *giving power to the tired*
> *and reviving the exhausted.*
> *Youths will become tired and weary,*
> *young men will certainly stumble;*
> *but those who hope in the LORD*
> *will renew their strength;*
> *they will fly up on wings like eagles;*

they will run and not be tired;
they will walk and not be weary.
(Isaiah 40:28-31)

I don't know what journeys you've been on that you did not want to take, or what journey you may be on now. I know that God walks with you. I know that God will strengthen you. I know that God redeems life's painful journeys.

Born in a Stable

Finally, Joseph and Mary arrived in Bethlehem. The way we usually imagine the story, upon arriving at the Bethlehem Inn they found that all the rooms were taken. Every AirBnB and VRBO was booked as well. Either a cruel innkeeper refused to care for them, or a compassionate innkeeper allowed Mary and Joseph to bed down among the animals in the barn behind the inn. Here Mary gave birth among the animals.

Now, it's likely that this story is partially right but in many ways wrong. Let's consider a few details. First, as we've learned, Joseph probably was from Bethlehem, so why would he need to stay at an inn? Second, Bethlehem was a small village in the first century, and so it's unlikely there was an inn; Jerusalem was nearby and would have provided public lodging. Third, people didn't have barns as we think of them. They did, however, frequently build their homes atop naturally occurring caves. When doing so, they often brought their animals into the caves at night or, if not into the caves, into the main common space in the home.

Let's remember precisely what Luke says in his account of Jesus' birth. Like Matthew's account, Luke's is surprisingly sparse.

> *He went to be enrolled together with Mary, who was promised to him in marriage and who was pregnant. While they were there, the time came for Mary to have her baby. She gave birth to her firstborn child, a son, wrapped him snugly, and laid him in a manger, because there was no place for them in the guestroom.*
>
> *(Luke 2:5-7)*

Notice that there is no mention of an old wooden barn. It doesn't state they arrived just as Mary was going into labor. And nothing is said about an inn or innkeeper. Now, to be fair, the word *inn* does show up in most English translations, but this is largely due to tradition. In these verses, the Greek word *kataluma* is more accurately translated as "guestroom," as we find it in the Common English Bible. The *kataluma* was the equivalent of a spare bedroom.*

The census would have brought most of Joseph's family to Bethlehem. We have no idea how many siblings and cousins were seeking to use that guestroom, but we can imagine that adding Joseph and Mary to a room already filled with people was not an option. First of all, childbirth made a room ritually "unclean" for a period of time, preventing the rest of the family from staying there if Mary gave birth in this space. Second, Mary would want and need her privacy while giving birth. And third, a midwife would have wanted space for the delivery.

Given these factors, it's likely that putting Mary and Joseph in the stable was an act of compassion; it could well have been another nudge of the Holy Spirit that led the family to clear out the stable so that Mary could have privacy as she gave birth without rendering the rest of the house ritually unclean. The earliest Christian tradition, dating back to the second century, notes that this stable was located in a cave, likely under Joseph's

---

* In the first century, a common layout in homes owned by working people of moderate means might have included one large bedroom, a common room that served as kitchen and living space, and a guestroom, often a loft or upper room built atop an exterior pen where the animals were kept if there was no cave beneath the home.

home. Christians still visit this cave when they come to Bethlehem, atop which sits the Church of the Nativity, the oldest continuously used church building in the world.

What is intended to be noticed in this story is the humility of the scene. The Savior of the world, the King of kings, the Son of God, was born in a stable where the animals were kept. His crib was a manger, a feeding trough for the animals, where the Bread of Life spent his first night on earth. There is something profound and beautiful in this story. Christians believe that in Jesus, God himself came to us. When God came, he chose to identify with the lowest and humblest of people. Jesus was born in the first-century equivalent of a parking garage or a shelter. I love this story, because it tells us so much about God, and it points to the character of Jesus' entire life—a life of humility and servanthood.

Luke's telling of the story continues the theme of humility with a visit by shepherds who were "keeping watch over their flock by night" (Luke 2:8 NRSV). Shepherds in that day were on the lowest rungs of the socioeconomic ladder. They were not often trusted. They were typically uneducated and poor and were held in low esteem by many. But on the night when Christ was born, who did God send the angels to invite so they could meet the newborn king? He invited shepherds! And not just any shepherds; he invited the night-shift shepherds, the lowest of the low.

Listen to what the angel announced to the shepherds. It's the same message we offer the world today as we approach Christmas.

> *The angel said, "Don't be afraid! Look! I bring good news to you—wonderful, joyous news for all people. Your savior is born today in David's city. He is Christ the Lord. This is a sign for you: you will find a newborn baby wrapped snugly and lying in a manger."*
>
> *(Luke 2:10-12)*

Good news. Wonderful, joyous news. *For all people.* Our savior, our deliverer, our King and Lord was born as a child, wrapped snugly and sleeping in a feeding trough for animals. From the start, God was teaching us through his Son and through the guests who came to celebrate the birth. What they saw in the child, if they really understood—and what we still find, if we really understand—is the glory of God revealed, and peace to all who see and understand and trust him. This is Christmas, when God has come near—in humility, as a child born in the humblest of ways, surrounded by Joseph, Mary, and the night-shift shepherds.

I am United Methodist, but I greatly admire Pope Francis. He is a remarkable figure. When the pope celebrated his eightieth birthday in 2016, he began his day with a special birthday breakfast. To help him celebrate, he invited eight homeless people to join him for the meal. I love that. Pope Francis acted in a way that embodied the character of God. When Christ was born, God invited night-shift shepherds, people who had no roof over their heads when they worked, to celebrate the birth.

Pope Francis offered an example for all Christians. If we overlook the message that God's good news came first to the lowly and the poor, then we have missed Luke's point. As Scripture says, "God opposes the proud, but gives grace to the humble" (1 Peter 5:5 NRSV). Jesus himself said, "So those who are last will be first. And those who are first will be last.... Whoever wants to be great among you will be your servant" (Matthew 20:16, 26).

These Scriptures offer a clear path forward. If we're to follow the Messiah who was born to a humble family in a lowly place, then we must open our eyes to the poor and marginalized. If we're in high school or middle school or elementary school, we're called to honor and lift up those who are picked on and unpopular. In the workplace we're to stand up for those who have been made to feel small. This is an important theme in Luke's telling of the Christmas story.

I'll end by returning to Joseph. Some of you reading this book are dads. Two of the most remarkable moments in my life were when my daughters, Danielle and Rebecca, were born.

Danielle was born December 22. After the pushing and pain and flurry of activity she was finally here, and after the nurses quickly cleaned her, they stuffed her in a Christmas stocking made by the United Methodist Women of Dallas for all the new babies being delivered at Methodist Hospital that week. Then they handed her to me. To hold that little girl for the first time, my heart was immediately filled with love for her, a love I didn't know could be so deep. I prayed and gave her to God, held her tight, then gave her back to my wife.

Three and a half years later I held our youngest, Rebecca, and once more felt overwhelming love for that beautiful little girl. Now, twenty-seven and thirty years later, I love them even more.

I feel sure that Joseph experienced the same emotions that night in Bethlehem when the midwife handed him

"Saint Joseph with the Infant Jesus" by Guido Reni

the baby Jesus, wrapped snugly. We can see those emotions in artist Guido Reni's "Saint Joseph with the Infant Jesus," painted around 1635. Though I believe Joseph was likely a young man rather than an old one as shown here, the tenderness in Joseph's face as he holds his son captures what I imagine Joseph was feeling that night.

God, how grateful we are that you never leave us or forsake us. Thank you for walking with us on our journeys in life, particularly the ones we don't want to take. Thank you for working through them and bringing good from them. Thank you for the Christmas story—for coming to us in the most humble of ways, and for inviting the night-shift shepherds to be the first to marvel at Christ's birth. Help us to trust in the "wonderful, joyous news for all people." Christ, I trust in you as my Deliverer, my King, and my Lord. Amen.

THE REST OF THE STORY

When eight days had passed, Jesus' parents circumcised him and gave him the name Jesus. This was the name given to him by the angel before he was conceived. When the time came for their ritual cleansing, in accordance with the Law from Moses, they brought Jesus up to Jerusalem to present him to the Lord. (It's written in the Law of the Lord, "Every firstborn male will be dedicated to the Lord.") They offered a sacrifice in keeping with what's stated in the Law of the Lord, A pair of turtledoves or two young pigeons.

(Luke 2:21-24)

THE REST OF THE STORY

As a pastor, I know there are all kinds of Christians. There are the Holy Day Christians that I see faithfully every Christmas and Easter. I'm always glad to welcome them, and I always hope this will be the year when something moves them to seek a deeper level of commitment. There are the fair-weather Christians. If the weather is not too bad (or for that matter not too nice) and if their favorite ball team is not playing within an hour of the time church will be out, there's a chance they'll join us for worship. There are the folks who are faithful in worship but never internalize the good news and it has little impact upon them. And then there are those whose faith runs deep, who daily offer their lives to Christ, who are being shaped by the Spirit; their lives reflect their faith in all that they do. Jesus spoke of all of these categories of believers in his parable of the sower.

What about Joseph? What kind of faith did he have? At every mention of Joseph in the stories surrounding the birth of Jesus, we see Joseph's faithfulness. Just to recap, Matthew tells us Joseph "was a righteous man" and recounts how Joseph demonstrated his compassion and mercy toward Mary in trying not to publicly humiliate her. After Joseph's dream in which the angel appeared to him, Joseph awoke and, rather than dismissing the dream, "he did just as an angel from God commanded and took Mary as his wife." In Luke's Gospel we learn that Joseph took Mary with him to Nazareth, likely to protect her and the child she carried despite the difficulty of the journey for both of them. In the weeks after Jesus' birth, Joseph once again demonstrated his faithfulness.

Circumcision and Dedication

Leviticus 12 gave directions to the Israelites regarding what was to happen after a child was born. On the eighth day after birth, male children were to be circumcised. A number of ancient cultures performed circumcision. God commanded Abraham and his descendants to be circumcised as "a symbol of the covenant between us" (Genesis 17:11) and a pledge by the parents to raise the child as a "son of the covenant."

In many ways, the Christian traditions that practice infant baptism see this act in a way similar to circumcision. In infant baptism God enters into a covenant with the child, and the parents, on the child's behalf, enter into a covenant with God. (Likewise, there is a parallel between the Jewish act of bar mitzvah and the Christian act of confirmation.) Both baptism and confirmation have a much larger range of meanings, but they share in common their being outward signs of a promise or covenant between God and the one being baptized or confirmed.

To the degree that contemporary practices of circumcision mirror the ancient practices, it is interesting to note that it's the father of the infant being circumcised who places the child into the hands of the individual who will hold the child during circumcision—the *sandek*, the father's representative. Then, during the ceremony, the father stands next to the *mohel*, the trained individual who will circumcise the child. The father hands the knife to the *mohel* and recites a blessing during the circumcision: "Blessed are You, Lord our God, King of the Universe, who has sanctified us with his commandments and commanded us to enter him into the Covenant of Abraham our Father."[1] We can't know if this is precisely how the circumcision took place in Joseph's day, but it may give us an idea of practices at that time and the father's role in the circumcision. I can picture Joseph standing next to his infant son during the circumcision and joining in the blessing for his son. Following this, Joseph would have named his son Jesus just as the angel had instructed in Joseph's dream.

In Luke 2:21-24, the passage at the beginning of this chapter, Luke describes the circumcision, cleansing, and dedication. Because of the way the passage is written, the reader may be left with the impression that all these actions occurred at the same time. But though the circumcision took place on the eighth day after the child was born, the ritual cleansing and dedication occurred some time later. When a woman gave birth to a boy, she was considered to be ceremonially unclean for forty days after his birth (the first seven days before circumcision plus another thirty-three days including the day of circumcision). Thus Luke's story of the baby Jesus' early days—his dedication at the temple, the blessings given the child by the elder Simeon and Anna, and Mary's offering for her purification—occurred forty days after Jesus' birth. Luke notes that Mary and Joseph offered a pair of turtledoves or pigeons, the sacrifice offered by those who were too poor to offer a lamb (Leviticus 12:8).

Luke's point in mentioning these events seems to be for his readers to understand that Joseph and Mary fulfilled the Law as all devout Jews would have done; Luke explicitly mentions this in 2:39: "Mary and Joseph...completed everything required by the Law of the Lord." These events show the kind of faith Joseph had, which will be demonstrated again several times before his story is concluded. Joseph truly was faithful.

The Coming of the Wise Men

At Christmas, Christians often focus on Luke's account of the Christmas story. But, as mentioned previously, if all we had was Luke's account of Jesus' birth, there is much we would be missing: the coming of the wise men, King Herod's attempt to kill the infant Jesus, the Holy Family's flight to Egypt. Instead of describing these events, Luke tells us that, immediately following Jesus' dedication at the temple, "Mary and Joseph...returned to their hometown, Nazareth in Galilee" (Luke 2:39). We are fortunate to have both Matthew and Luke for the different birth and infancy traditions each Gospel preserves. Each gives us a slightly different view of Jesus' early life, which helps us imagine Joseph's role in the story.

Just as Luke doesn't mention the wise men, Matthew doesn't mention the visit of the humble night-shift shepherds. While Matthew agrees with Luke about Jesus' concern for the lowly, he emphasizes that Jesus came to express God's love and mercy not only for the poor, but also for the rich. Jesus came not just for the uneducated but for the educated. He came not just for the Jews but for the entire world.

Matthew wants to make it clear that Jesus was not simply the Jewish messiah but the *world's* savior and king. We can see this emphasis from the beginning of the Gospel, as the magi from the east come to pay homage to the infant Christ and bow down before him. Matthew ends his Gospel with this same theme, with Jesus giving the Great Commission: "Go and make disciples of *all nations*, baptizing them in the name of the Father and of the Son and of the Holy Spirit, teaching them to obey everything that I've commanded you" (Matthew 28: 19-20, *emphasis added*).

Regarding the visit of the magi, here is how Matthew introduces the story:

> *After Jesus was born in Bethlehem in the*
> *territory of Judea during the rule of King Herod,*
> *magi came from the east to Jerusalem. They*
> *asked, "Where is the newborn king of the Jews?*

We've seen his star in the east, and we've come to honor him."

(Matthew 2:1-2)

Most likely, the magi came from Persia. By the way, *magi* is the root of our word "magician." These magi probably were not magicians in the way we think of that term. They were likely part of the priestly class within the Zoroastrian religion—respected court advisors, scholars, sages, devout believers in God, and scientists of a sort. They studied the stars and looked to them for signs of God's plans and world events. They were astrologers in a time when astrologers were not simply creators of horoscopes but students of the stars. Zoroastrianism originated in Persia (modern-day Iran) possibly in the late seventh or early sixth century before Christ. The prophet Zoroaster was to Zoroastrianism what Moses was to Judaism. Both religions shared a belief in one good and all-powerful God, in a host of other theological ideas, and in common ethical imperatives. Yet they were as different from one another as, say, Judaism is from Islam.

This is why I find the visit of the magi so remarkable. According to Matthew, God intentionally chose to invite a group of foreigners, priests of a different religion, to share in the joy of Jesus' birth. And God used them to provide what would prove to be much-needed help for the Holy Family.

In response to their sighting of the star and their deduction that a king of the Jews had been born, these wise men, who were not Jews, traveled twelve hundred miles across the ancient highways from Persia to Judea in order to see the child, bring him gifts, and pay him homage. What does that tell us about the depth of their faith and the broadness of their understanding of God's providence?

Picking up Matthew's story, the magi followed the star to Jerusalem where they asked, "Where is the newborn king of the Jews? We've seen his star in the east, and we've come to honor him" (Matthew 2:2). Their arrival and announcement of a newborn king unnerved the aging and paranoid King Herod. (Over the years, he'd had three of his sons executed for fear they were attempting to take his throne.) Herod, quite anxious to find the child, called for the chief priests and legal experts to find out where the Scriptures foretold the Messiah would be born. The priests pointed out Micah's words, that a messianic ruler was to come from Bethlehem. Herod sent the magi to Bethlehem to search for the child, saying, "When you've found him, report to me so that I too may go and honor him" (2:8). Matthew continues,

When they heard the king, they went; and look,
the star they had seen in the east went ahead
of them until it stood over the place where the
child was. When they saw the star, they were
filled with joy. They entered the house and saw
the child with Mary his mother. Falling to their
knees, they honored him. Then they opened their
treasure chests and presented him with gifts of
gold, frankincense, and myrrh.

(Matthew 2:9-11)

Imagine what Joseph must have been thinking when an entourage of court officials and priests from the far east showed up at the door of his very humble home. What must have been going through his mind as he watched the wise men, one by one, open their extravagant gifts and bow before Joseph's infant son, hailing him as the one "born king of the Jews"?

Matthew likely saw the connection of this event to Isaiah's prophecies:

Nations will come to your light
  and kings to your dawning radiance....
They will all come...
  carrying gold and incense,
  proclaiming the LORD's praises.

(Isaiah 60:3, 6)

It is from this connection between the visit of the magi and Isaiah 60 that the church began to think of the magi as kings, which in turn gave us the wonderful carol "We Three Kings."

At times, religious people can be pretty full of themselves. (This is true of all religious people, even those whose religion is atheism.) We Christians can be so smugly certain that we know the truth, and that those who don't agree are not only wrong but damned. However, right here at the beginning of the gospel story we find God doing something that really messes with our theology.

I wonder if this story might teach us, at the very least, to treat those of other faiths the way God honored the magi. Or perhaps we might learn to treat those of other faiths with respect and honor, as the magi did the Jews in bringing their gifts to the newborn king. Learning these lessons might be part of the key to experiencing "peace on earth, good will to all people."

I have friends who are adherents of other religions, and some who reject religion altogether. Rather than constantly trying to convert them, I've sought to do what God did with the magi, to befriend them and be befriended by them. I'm sure that you, too, have neighbors of other faiths, or of no faith. I think God is pleased when we treat others with respect, and when we listen to them and learn from them, even as we share our own faith with gentleness, respect, and humility.

I don't believe all faiths are equally valid, or simply different ways of saying the same thing. That doesn't honor any faith. But I do believe that in most faiths there are points of connection and there are people earnestly seeking to find the light of God's love and grace. My hope is to be a great witness and representative of Christ, and to love and show grace as God did with the magi.

Joseph, Mary, and Jesus as Refugees

When the magi left, they, like Joseph, had a dream in which God spoke to them. In the dream they were warned not to return to their home country through Jerusalem but to return by another route. In Jerusalem, remember, Herod was waiting for news of the child's birth and hatching a plan to kill him. So the magi heeded the warning and returned to Persia.

We've talked about why the magi came, but it's not clear how long after Jesus' birth they arrived. The Christian church has celebrated the coming of the magi at Epiphany, which is observed in many churches on January 6. But if I were to try to reconcile Matthew's account of the Nativity with Luke's, I would suggest the wise men came after Jesus' dedication in the temple. This would mean at least six weeks after Christ's birth. But it may have been much longer than that.

It would have taken at least sixty days to make the journey from Persia to Bethlehem, though the magi could have seen the star before Jesus was born. Herod's decision, upon realizing that the magi were not returning to Jerusalem with information regarding the child, to kill every boy child in Bethlehem under two years of age "according to the time that he had learned from the magi" (Matthew 2:16) might tell us that the magi didn't arrive until Jesus was a year old or even older. In any event, it is not likely that the wise men were there at Jesus' birth, along with the shepherds, as is usually portrayed in our Nativity sets.

Once again Joseph, like his namesake in the Book of Genesis, heard God speak in his dreams. God warned Joseph to take Mary and Jesus and flee to Egypt because Herod would soon be coming to look for Jesus. Joseph gathered his little family, and they made the journey to Egypt—what is usually described as "the flight to Egypt." This would have been a several-hundred-mile trip along the coastal highway. How did they have the means to make this trip and then survive once they were in Egypt? It was the gifts of the magi, gifts that helped save the lives of the Holy Family.

I was in Egypt recently and had the opportunity to visit one of the many churches associated with the Holy Family's sojourn in that country. Hippolytus of Rome, writing in his commentary on Matthew early in the third century, suggested that Joseph, Mary, and Jesus remained in Egypt for three and a half years. Outside of Egypt, it's often thought that the family remained in Egypt for less than a year, returning to the Holy Land shortly after Herod's death.

What I find interesting and moving, in the light of various refugee crises around the world and particularly the Syrian refugee crisis, is that the infant Jesus was himself a refugee. His family, like many of today's refugees, fled the brutality of a despot who had no compunction about putting to death anyone he deemed a threat. The same cruelty we see at the hands of despots today was at play in the stories surrounding Christ's birth.

King Herod sent troops to kill the male children under the age of two in Bethlehem. Bethlehem was a small village at that time, inhabited by anywhere from several hundred to one thousand people. How many were boys under the age of two? Was it a dozen? Several dozen? We can't know. What we do know is that even in the midst of the Christmas story we find the reality of the world's brokenness.

The United Nations High Commission on Refugees noted recently that there are now over sixty-five million people in the world who have been forced to leave their homes.[2] I recently sat with a Syrian refugee family that had immigrated to the United States, with an Iraqi refugee as my interpreter, seeking to hear their story.

The Syrian family described fleeing their country because the government stopped allowing their daughters to have the blood transfusions needed to keep them alive. As the father described the day he left Syria with his family, he began to weep. He told me he would never forget that day. His wife began to weep. Our interpreter, who was forced to flee his country, began to weep. I was deeply moved as I heard the father describe the pain of leaving behind family, friends, and home in order to save the lives of his children. I listened as the interpreter described his own family who had died back in his home country.

These people did not want to leave their home countries. They hadn't dreamed of coming to America. In the case of this father, he was willing to go wherever he had to go and do whatever he had to do in order to save his family. As these men wept in my presence, I wondered if the response wouldn't have been similar if I had been sitting in Egypt two thousand years ago, listening to Joseph and Mary describe their flight from Bethlehem. As I listened to this Syrian father, I saw the face of Joseph.

I remembered that Jesus, who had been a refugee, once told his disciples that the final judgment would be based on how they—and we—choose to treat the hungry, the thirsty, the naked, *the stranger*, the sick, and the imprisoned. In oft-repeated words, Jesus said, "Just as you did it to one of the least of these…you did it to me" (Matthew 25:40 NRSV).

Just as St. Teresa saw Jesus in the suffering poor of Calcutta, I believe we're meant to see Jesus in the refugees who flee political or religious persecution and threat of death.

Return to Galilee and the Childhood of Jesus

King Herod's death is usually dated at 4 BC but sometimes at 1 BC.* Matthew tells us:

> *After King Herod died, an angel from the Lord appeared in a dream to Joseph in Egypt. "Get up," the angel said, "and take the child and his*

---

* You can read some of the debate about whether Herod's death was in 4 BC or 1 BC at http://www.biblicalarchaeology.org/daily/people -cultures-in-the-bible/jesus-historical-jesus/herods-death-jesus-birth -and-a-lunar-eclipse/.

mother and go to the land of Israel. Those who were trying to kill the child are dead." Joseph got up, took the child and his mother, and went to the land of Israel.

(Matthew 2:19-21)

It appears that Joseph initially planned to return to Judea but was warned in a dream not to go there, so "he settled in a city called Nazareth" (v. 23).

The biblical Gospels tell us nothing else about Jesus' childhood, with the exception of a wonderful little story in Luke 2:41-52, when Jesus was twelve years old. The story begins, "Each year his parents went to Jerusalem for the Passover Festival." This statement points once again to Joseph and Mary's faithfulness. They took Jesus to Jerusalem for the feast. But we read nothing more about the feast. Instead we learn that when everyone from Galilee was returning home among a large band of travelers, there was a mix-up. Joseph thought Jesus was with Mary; Mary thought Jesus was with Joseph. They traveled a day's journey before they realized that neither of them had Jesus; in fact, he was nowhere to be found.

Joseph and Mary hurried back to Jerusalem searching for their son, and it wasn't until the third day that they found him. He was in the temple courts, sitting among the teachers and asking them questions, and everyone listening to the boy was amazed. However, amazement was the last thing Joseph and Mary felt; they were shocked and undoubtedly angry. I love that we have Mary's words in that moment: "Child, why have you treated us like this? Listen! Your father and I have been worried. We've been looking for you!" (Luke 2:48). Jesus responded as only a twelve-year-old could: "Why were you looking for me? Didn't you know that it was necessary for me to be in my Father's house?" (Luke 2:49).

Did you ever wonder how Joseph felt when Jesus spoke these words? Did he say, "Wait, *I'm* your father"? Was he hurt by his twelve-year-old son, to whom he had given everything and for whom he had risked everything? Or did he think to himself, "He finally understands"? We can't know. What the story does tell us is that Joseph's love for Jesus could be seen in his worry and in his frantic search for the child. What it also tells us is that Jesus must have learned his lesson, because Luke writes, "Jesus went down to Nazareth with them and was obedient to them" (Luke 2:51).

The incident at the temple was Joseph's final appearance in the story of Jesus. We'll see that Mary was there when Jesus was crucified. She was at the Resurrection. She was in the Upper Room at Pentecost when the Spirit fell upon the fledgling Christian community. But Joseph would not appear again. He would be mentioned, as in Matthew 13:54-55, a text we looked at previously: When Jesus preached in the synagogue at Nazareth, the townspeople rejected him asking, "Where did he get this wisdom? Where did he get the power to work miracles? Isn't he the carpenter's son?" But by this time Joseph may well have been dead for some time. However, Joseph's profession as the town carpenter—repairing farm tools, building yokes for oxen, making or repairing furniture—was still somehow seen as making him incapable of producing a prophet or rabbi.

Several years ago as I was studying Joseph's life in Scripture, it struck me that Joseph never has any lines. We hear Mary speak. In many ways, between the two parents, Mary shines. She is the star of this story. Throughout church history this has been true. Yet how important was Joseph's role in Jesus' life? And what kind of influence did Joseph have on the Savior of the world? Joseph may be the patron saint of doubters, as I suggested earlier, but he's also the patron saint of those who work behind the scenes with little or no credit, yet whose impact is incalculable and so critical to God's work.

As a pastor I'm often in the limelight, preaching or leading. I get plenty of accolades (and a fair share of criticism). But there are so many people who don't stand in the limelight whose impact is incalculable. They don't do what they do to be recognized but do it because they feel called. These are the Josephs of the world.

The Death of Joseph

Joseph must have died sometime when Jesus was a young man. The Gospels tell us nothing about this event—their stories are largely focused on Jesus' public ministry that began when he was around the age of thirty—but we can, as later Christians did, surmise that Jesus was with Joseph at his death. I've been with many people as they died, and the closer I was to them emotionally, the harder their death was to accept. My father-in-law died several years ago. We spoke to him on the phone as the time was drawing near. Through our tears we said that we loved him, and then we quickly loaded the car and drove all night from Kansas City to central Illinois in the hope of seeing him before he died. When we arrived at the hospital, he had just died. We sat by his side, weeping, praying, and telling him of our love for him, then we gave him to God. Would Jesus not have felt that same pain at the death of the man who raised him as his own son?

Did Jesus hold Joseph near as he was dying? Did he offer Joseph words of encouragement and compassion, promising him, "My Father's house has room to spare"? Did he whisper as his father died, "I am the resurrection and the life....Everyone who lives and believes in me will never die" or "I have the keys of Death and the Grave, and because I live, you will live too"?

In *The History of Joseph the Carpenter*, an apocryphal book mentioned in chapter 1, Jesus purportedly held a conversation with his disciples, telling them about Joseph. Much of the conversation was focused on Joseph's death. Though Jesus' words were a product of a pious imagination and were built upon traditions that came before, they painted a beautiful picture of how Christians at the time imagined Joseph's death.

In the account, as Joseph was dying, Jesus sat at his bedside, holding Joseph's hand. Mary sat on the other side of the bed, holding his other hand. Joseph's other children, assumed to be from a previous marriage, moved in and out of the room, weeping over their father.

Joseph fixed his eyes on Jesus' face. Though Joseph couldn't speak, he wept. Then Jesus prayed to God for Joseph, that God would send the great angels Michael and Gabriel to welcome his father to heaven. The two came, just as Jesus had requested, and took the soul of Joseph. Jesus, lying across Joseph's breast, "bewailed his death for a long time." The scene may well reflect the kind of sorrow Jesus felt as he bid his father goodbye.

Playing Hide-and-Seek with God

I've known a great deal of joy in my life, and a bit of sorrow as well. I know the joy of God's grace and love and am grateful for it each day. I know the love of a wife with whom I've shared life for more than thirty-five years. But among the greatest joys in my life is being a father to Danielle and Rebecca, and now grandfather to our granddaughter Stella.

I never knew how deeply I could love another human being until my daughters were born. And now, with our granddaughter, I feel that remarkable love all over again. I can't help thinking that Joseph felt the same love for Jesus. And I'm convinced that the love I feel for my children and grandchild is a reflection of the love God has for us.

As I conclude this book on Joseph and the meaning of Christmas, I'd like to share a story about Stella. As I write this, she is three years old. Once or twice a month, Stella comes to our home and spends the night. Her favorite game is hide-and-seek, or as she calls it, "Come Find Me." She says to me, "Papa, come find me."

Usually what she really means is "Mimi, come find me," because she wants me to hide with her. We'll hide behind a door, or in the pantry, or beside the bed. LaVon will count to ten and search for us, saying, "Where's Stella? Where's Papa?" At that point, Stella will start giggling and squealing. I'll whisper to her, "Shhhh!" But she giggles all the more. Even so, LaVon will pretend she doesn't know where we are. Finally Stella will giggle and squeal again, and LaVon will find us.

Then she and Mimi will hide, and I will be the seeker. When I find them, Stella shrieks for joy all over again. She would happily play this game for hours!

The thing is, *Stella wants to be found.* For her, that's the whole point of the game. And when we find her, she shrieks with delight and hugs her Mimi and Papa. It fills her with joy to be found. She wants to be safe in her grandparents' arms.

Somehow I think that's what Christmas is all about. Ultimately, Christmas was God's way of coming to find us and to be found by us. We sometimes run from God. We pretend God can't see us. We pretend God isn't there. But all the while, somewhere deep down inside, I think we want to be found, and we want to find God.

At Christmas God came to us in a way that we can understand, with human flesh and bone, so helpless that first Christmas, and so beautiful, that shepherds and magi took delight in seeing him.

When Jesus grew up, he announced that he had come to seek and to save those who are lost. His ministry was devoted to searching for those who have strayed or are hiding from God. He spent himself, and ultimately laid down his life, to show the human race what his Father was really like. The invisible God came in Jesus to find and to be found.

I wonder, did Joseph play hide-and-seek with Jesus? Did Jesus shriek with joy when Joseph found him? I wonder if Joseph wasn't teaching Jesus all the while: No matter where you go, no matter how well you hide, you have another Father who will always look for you and find you, whose love will never let you go. Son, that's why you are here, why God blessed me with you, so that you can show the world this truth, and so that all people might find and be found by God.

This is the gift of Christmas: being found and finding, being held and holding, being safe in God's arms and being saved by God's arms. I wonder if Jesus didn't first experience this gift in the loving arms of Joseph.

Lord, at times we feel lost. At times we feel afraid. Come find us. Hold us close. Thank you for coming so that, as you find us, we might find you. Dry our tears. Comfort us. Save us. Thank you for Joseph, whose life and faith are a picture of faithfulness and whose love guarded and shaped you, Jesus, that you might shape us. Thank you, Lord, for Joseph. Amen.

NOTES

1. A Carpenter Named Joseph

1. See Wesley's "Letter to a Roman Catholic," section 7, subparagraph 3—this was written in 1749.
2. Justin Martyr, *Dialogue with Trypho*, chapter 88, in *Ante-Nicene Fathers*, vol. 1 (Christian Literature Publishing Co., 1885), 244.
3. Paul C. Vitz, *Faith of the Fatherless: The Psychology of Atheism* (Dallas: Spence Publishing, 1999), 16.
4. Ibid.
5. This statistic comes from a poll commissioned by Strobel for his book *The Case for Grace: A Journalist Explores the Evidence of Transformed Lives* (Grand Rapids, MI: Zondervan, 2015).

2. Whose Child Is This?

1. Ron Chernow, *Alexander Hamilton* (New York: Penguin Press, 2004), 5.
2. Michael Gungor and Lisa Gungor, "Beautiful Things," from the album *Beautiful Things* (Brash Records, 2010).
3. I'm indebted to Hayyim Schauss, who taught for twenty-five years at the Jewish Teachers Seminary in New York, and his article here on My Jewish Learning: http://www.myjewishlearning.com /article/ancient-jewish-marriage/.

3. Raising a Child Not Your Own

1. Children's Bureau of the Administration for Children and Families (U.S. Department of Health and Human Services), "Trends in Foster Care and Adoption" (June 30, 2016; https://www.acf.hhs .gov/cb/resource/trends-in-foster-care-and-adoption-fy15).

2. Amy Dworsky and Mark Courtney. "Assessing the Impact of Extending Care beyond Age 18 on Homelessness: Emerging Findings from the Midwest Study." Chicago: Chapin Hall, 2010. http://www.chapinhall.org/sites/default/files/publications /Midwest_IB2_Homelessness. Accessed July 10, 2017.

4. The Journey to Bethlehem

1 Josephus Nelson Larned, *The New Larned History for Ready Reference, Reading and Research...*, vol. 2 (Springfield, MA: C.A. Nichols Publishing, 1922), 1491.

2. If you'd like to read about Aleem Maqbool's journey or watch video of his travel, visit the BBC website at http://news.bbc.co .uk/2/hi/middle_east/7784227.stm.

The Rest of the Story

1. Malka Z. Simkovich. "Abraham as the Great (Un)Circumciser: A Surprising Midrashic Portrait of Abraham." TheTorah.com. http:// thetorah.com/abraham-circumcision/. Accessed July 11, 2017.

2. Adrian Edwards. "Forced displacement worldwide at its highest in decades." UNHCR–The UN Refugee Agency. http://www .unhcr.org/en-us/news/stories/2017/6/5941561f4/forced -displacement-worldwide-its-highest-decades.html. Published June 19, 2017. Accessed July 11, 2017.

ACKNOWLEDGMENTS

I am sincerely grateful to the team at Abingdon Press for making this book possible. From the initial concept of preparing a book on Joseph, to their work in helping me transform an Advent sermon series into a book, to the coordination of a small group study for all ages, the Abingdon team has played a critical role in the publication of this book.

I specifically want to thank Susan Salley for her friendship and for serving as a great sounding board and conversation partner in hashing out the ideas in this book and other of my books. I'm grateful for Ron Kidd, whose editorial skills and publishing sensibilities are a gift to me and elevate the quality and readability of my books. Thank you, Ron.

Thanks to Randy Horick, who helped me with early drafts of the book; to Tim Cobb and Marcia Myatt, who oversaw production and art; to the video teams at the United Methodist Church of the Resurrection and United Methodist Communications; to Alan Vermilye, who supervised the marketing; and to the many others at Abingdon and beyond who helped produce this book and program.

As always, I'm grateful to the people of the United Methodist Church of the Resurrection. It is in the context of my ministry with you that the ideas in this book take on flesh. I am honored to be your pastor.

Finally, I want to thank my wife, LaVon; my daughters, Danielle and Rebecca; my son-in-law, J. T.; and my granddaughter, Stella, for their love and the many ways they inspire me.

CPSIA information can be obtained
at www.ICGtesting.com
Printed in the USA
LVOW10s0154031117

554798LV00005B/9/P